World Chronology Series

THE NETHERLANDS
A CHRONOLOGY AND FACT BOOK

57 B.C. - 1971

Compiled and Edited by
PAMELA and J. W. SMIT

1973
OCEANA PUBLICATIONS, INC.
Dobbs Ferry, New York

Library of Congress Cataloging in Publication Data

Smit, Pamela.
    The Netherlands.

    (World chronology series no. 1)
    1. Netherlands -- History -- Chronology.
2. Belgium -- History -- Chronology. I. Smit,
Jacobus Wilheminus, joint author. II. Title.
III. Series.
DH101.S5   949.2   73-5599
ISBN 0-379-16301-2

Manufactured in the United States of America

TABLE OF CONTENTS

INTRODUCTION.   v

CHRONOLOGY
    Roman Period and Early Middle Ages   1
    The Feudal Principalities.   2
    Unification Under the Burgundian and Habsburg Dynasties
        (1369-1555)   4
    The Dutch Revolution (1566-1609).   11
    The Emergence of the Dutch Republic (1609-1648).   18
    The Dutch Republic as a Great Power (1648-1748)   23
    The Decline of the Republic and the Period of Democratic
        Revolution and French Occupation (1748-1813).   34
    Liberation and Establishment of the Kingdom of the
        Netherlands, (1813-1848)   39
    The Establishment of Parliamentary Monarchy (1840-1868) . .   44
    The Growth of the Modern Party-State: Economic Revival
        (1868-1914)   46
    Between the World Wars (1918-1939)   51
    The Second World War (1940-1945).   55
    After World War Two (1945-1959)   57
    The Unruly Sixties and Seventies.   62
    Stadtholders and Sovereigns of the House of Orange.   65
    Family Tree of the Sovereigns of the House of Orange-
        Nassau   66
    Cabinets in the Netherlands Since 1848.   67

DOCUMENTS
    I   The Dutch National Anthem   71
    II Report of the Riots of Antwerp, 1566   73
    III William of Orange's Speech to the Assembly of the
        States General, 1576.   75
    IV The Bill of Abjuration, 1581   76
    V   The Itinerario of Jan Van Linschoten, 1598   79
    VI Diary of a Seaman, Arctic Voyage   81
    VII Excerpts from Pieter de la Court's The Interest of
        Holland, 1662   85
    VIII Manifesto of the Democratic Movement, 1781.   89
    IX Lord Castlereagh's Memorandum to the Allies Concerning
        the Netherlands, 1813   90
    X   Proclamation Establishing Monarchy in the Netherlands,
        1813.   93
    XI An English View of the Dutch Parliament in 1860   94
    XII Queen Wilhelmina's Description of the Beginning of
        World War II, 1940   99

XIII Description of Amsterdam's Anti-Persecution Strike,
    1941 101
XIV Queen Wilhelmina's Description of the Liberation,
    1944-1945 103
  XV The Damages of the Second World War, 1945 108
XVI Documents Concerning the Dutch-Indonesian Conflict,
    1945-1949. 123
Sources of Documents 147

INDEX. 149

INTRODUCTION

The history of Holland, or more properly, the Netherlands, has a significance far beyond its present modest position in the world. For many generations, particularly of Americans, the sixteenth century Revolt of the Netherlands meant the first example in European history of emancipation from the forces of tyranny and spiritual oppression, and the subsequent history of the Dutch Republic seemed to exemplify the reign of toleration and enlightenment as well as that of economic enterprise and prowess.

The real history of the Netherlands is more complicated than the idealized picture of, for example, the famous American historian John Motley. It always is. There is much to be detracted from the idealism and toleration of the founders of the Dutch state, and its economic prowess was often ruthless empire-building. In spite of much justified criticism though, it is also true that Dutch history still stands as an inspiring example of human endeavor, worthy to be known to posterity.

Among the peculiarities of Dutch history are the difficulties of delimiting its scope in time and area. Around the middle of the sixteenth century, the present-day Netherlands, Belgium, Luxemburg and Northwest France were part of the same Habsburg government. It is incorrect, therefore, to begin Dutch history with the sixteenth century revolt against the Habsburg Empire from which the Republic emerged. Long before that time, a Netherlands culture had been flourishing, whose center lay outside the boundaries of the later Dutch Republic. Dutch was and is spoken and written in the largest part of Belgium, and in the towns of Ghent, Brugge, Antwerp and Brussels that culture found its richest expression. But the French-speaking parts of present-day Belgium also shared the typical Netherlands form of urban life and bourgeois culture which later became the hallmark of the Dutch Republic.

Ironically, the Revolt of the Netherlands which created the Dutch Republic insured at the same time the permanent secession of those southern provinces, when the revolutionary forces were defeated there.

Aside from a few attempts to recover Belgium in the seventeenth century and an unsuccessful reunion from 1815-1830, we have to accept the fact that two different states had grown up in the territory of the once so promising seventeen Netherlands provinces.

The following chronology acknowledges these facts by sketching the medieval history and growth of the provincial units which in the fifteenth and sixteenth century are gathered under one government by the Burgundian dukes and the Habsburg princes. Many of the high points in the Great Revolt against the despotism of Philip II of Habsburg, who was also the king of Spain, took place in the South. After the fall of Antwerp (1585), however, the leader of the Revolt, William of Orange, concentrated on the defense of the northern provinces, whose power was based on the province of Holland. When they finally become free, the liberation was won with the help of tens of thousands of refugees from the South, who also played a part in the amazing rise of the Dutch Republic in the seventeenth century.

The history of the Republic is highlighted by several persistent characteristics. On the political level, there is the ongoing battle between the Republican merchant government, mainly in the province of Holland, and the descendants of the Founding Father, William of Orange, who try to expand their power and impose more unity. On the religious level we see the battle between orthodox and liberal Calvinists. The politico-religious strife results in three coup d'etats by the Orange Stadtholders. Twice the leader of the Republicans had to die for his convictions, which have so deeply influenced Dutch mentality.

The decline of the Republic in the eighteenth century caused new, democratic ideas to become the program of the Patriot party, inspired by the American Revolution. After the French invasion, new concepts about national unification were tried which, after Napoleon's defeat, were incorporated into Dutch history by the elevation of the Oranges to royal dignity. The important themes of nineteenth century history are, then, the failure of the union with Belgium, the battle for constitutional rights of Parliament and the establishment of the peculiar Dutch party system, largely the result of religious and educational problems.

In the twentieth century a new Netherlands emerged, again conscious of a new international role in advocating peace, internationalism and neutrality; the German invasion of 1940 brutally ended that period. Of the two main themes after 1945, one will indeed be the adoption of an active diplomacy in alliance with the Western democracies; the other one is the gradual building of the welfare state through social legislation. The most recent years in Dutch politics have shown that in both these field several old and many new problems have yet to be solved.

ROMAN PERIOD AND EARLY MIDDLE AGES

57 B.C. The conquest of the Southern Netherlands by Julius
     Caesar. Caesar's reports constitute the first written
     source of Netherlands history. The Netherlands as far
     north as the Rhine was made part of the Roman province
     of Gaul in 51 B.C.

69-70   Revolt of the Batavi, a river delta tribe, against the
A.D.   Romans. This revolt took cn symbolic meaning during
     the events of the Revolt of the Netherlands in the 16th
     century, with the Batavian leader Julius Civilis being re-
     vered as a prefiguration of William of Orange.

406   The traditional date of the Germanic invasion of the pro-
     vince of Gaul which brought to an end Roman authority
     over the Netherlands.

c.500   At this time, at the beginning of the period of the Great
     Migrations, the Netherlands was inhabited by the Fris-
     ians, the Franks and the Saxons. The Frisians dwelled
     along the coast from the Zwin in Flanders in the south to
     the mouth of the Weser in Germany; the Franks lived in-
     land to the south of the great rivers and the Saxons inhab-
     ited the Eastern Netherlands.

689   Pippin II, steward of the Merovingian king of France,
     conquers the Frisian King Radbod. This brings the
     Netherlands within the Merovingian-Carolingian realm.
     It was Pippin II who sponsored the efforts of Willibrord,
     an Anglo-Saxon monk who arrived at the Rhine in 690, to
     evangelize the Low Countries. Willibrord was made
     bishop of the Frisians by the Pope in 695, whereupon he
     chose Utrecht as his seat.

785   Widukind, king of the Saxons, surrenders to Charlemagne,
     bringing the east and north of the Netherlands under
     Carolingian power.

843-
870
Division of the Carolingian Empire. After several division treaties among Charlemagne's descendants, most of
the Netherlands are given to the East Francian (German)
Empire; only Flanders falls to the West Francian Empire
(France).

THE FEUDAL PRINCIPALITIES

In the 10th and 11th centuries noblemen began founding feudal principali-
ties which were to become the basis of the later Netherlands provinces.
The most important of these would be the duchies of Brabant and
Guelders, the counties of Flanders and Holland, and the bishopric of
Utrecht. This period also witnessed the founding of many towns, the
most striking phenomenon of the Netherlands.

1007
The last attack of the Vikings upon the Netherlands. The
Vikings (mainly Danes) had begun their raids on the Low
Countries around 800.

1024
The German king gives the county of Drenthe to Bishop
Adalbold of Utrecht.

1056
Count Boudewijn of Flanders is officially granted as an
imperial fief all the land east of the Scheld and in present-
day Zeeland that he had claimed. Since that time one
distinguishes this Imperial Flanders from Crown Flanders,
which Boudewijn held as a vassal of the French king.

c. 1100
The beginning of wide-spread building of sea- and polder-
dikes where it was necessary. Polder authorities were
organized for the defense and maintenance of the dikes;
these authorities were frequently set up by the local
feudal lord.

c. 1113
The German Archbishop of Hamburg gives a group of
Netherlanders a tract of his marshlands for drainage.
This is the beginning of the participation by the Dutch in
the colonization of Eastern Germany.

1128
Gent and other Flemish cities proclaim Diederich of
Alsace count of Flanders in opposition to the ruling count.
Following Diederich's victory, the cities assume a more
important position than the nobles in Flanders.

1247   Count William II of Holland was elected King of the
            Romans.

1280   Social strife in the Flemish textile cities. The battles
            between the craft guilds and the patricians foreshadows
            the victory of the industrial guilds over the merchant
            patriciate in the 14th century.

1281   Revolt in Bruges against Count Guy of Dampierre, who had
            been trying with only partial success to bring the Flemish
            cities under control.

1289   Final subjugation of West Frisia by Count Floris V of
            Holland.

1300   Count Guy of Flanders, who had been trying to resist the
            authority of his feudal lord, the king of France, finally
            surrenders to King Philip IV of France.

1302   Battle of the Golden Spurs. The Flemish cities defeat the
            army of the French king, including its noble cavalry. The
            victory is an example of the growing power of the bour-
            geoisie. It was an inspiration for the towns of the Nether-
            lands, and, in the 19th century, for the cause of Flemish
            nationalism.

1305   First documented gathering of the Three Members of
            Flanders, the representatives of the three great cities,
            Bruges, Gent and Ypres. The Three Members become the
            core of the representative body of Flanders.

1306   Amsterdam receives its city charter from Bishop Gwyde
            of Utrecht.

1312   The Charter of Kortenberg is proclaimed by Duke John II
            of Brabant. This charter, which provides for a council
            composed of representatives of the nobility and the cities,
            is important for the evolution towards constitutional
            government in the Netherlands.

1323-   Rebellion of the yeoman farmers of coastal Flanders;
1328   anti-noble and anti-French sentiment were important
            factors.

1340	Edward III of England proclaimed King of France at Gent with the support of the Flemish towns.
1350	The Black Death sweeps Europe, leaving only some parts of the Netherlands untouched.
1356	Johanna of Brabant proclaims the constitution of the "Joyeuse Entree", giving the Estates of Brabant far-reaching privileges and promising that she would keep the duchy unified.
1360-1364	Pieter Coutereel brings the guilds into the city government at Louvain. In other Brabant cities as well the power of the patricians begins to fade, as Duke Wenceslas of Brabant is not in a position to give them as much support as his predecessors had done.
1362	A new constitution is drawn up by the Estates of Holland, Hainaut and Zeeland at Breda, giving the Estates a considerable role.

UNIFICATION UNDER THE BURGUNDIAN AND HABSBURG DYNASTIES (1369-1555)

1369	Marriage of Philip the Bold, Duke of Burgundy, to Margaretha, heiress of Lodewyck of Male, Count of Flanders. As a sign of recognition, the French king returns the area of French Flanders.
1379-1385	Great rebellion of Gent against the centralizing tendencies of the Flemish count. In 1382 the rebels were beaten at Westrozebeke. In 1386 at the peace of Doornik Philip the Bold's succession as count of Flanders is the beginning of the Burgundian dynasty which would ultimately unite most of the Netherlands under its rule.
1396	Duchess Johanna of Brabant gives Limburg and Outre-Meuse to Philip the Bold of Burgundy, whose son Antoon she had secretly declared heir to Brabant in return for Burgundian support.
1411	Antoon, Duke of Brabant, takes Luxenburg in the name of his wife, Elizabeth of Gorlitz.

1415	Jacoba, the only legitimate child of Count William VI of Holland, marries Prince John of Touraine, the apparent heir to the throne of France.
1417	Death of the Dauphin, John of Touraine, the husband of Jacoba of Bavaria, heiress of Holland. Jacoba's father, William VI, died one and a half months later.
1418	Jacoba of Bavaria marries the 15-year-old Duke John IV of Brabant.
1420	Treaty of St. Maartendsdyk op Tholen, whereby John of Bavaria is given the counties of Holland and Zeeland for twelve years.
1421	Jacoba of Bavaria, claiming the invalidity of her marriage to John of Brabant, flees to England, where in 1422 she marries Humphrey of Gloucester right after the death of his brother, King Henry V.
1425	Death of Duke John of Bavaria. Duke John IV of Brabant named Philip the Good of Burgundy as regent of Holland and Zeeland. The Duke of Gloucester, challenged to a duel by Philip, deserts Jacoba and flees to England, whereupon Jacoba becomes the prisoner of Philip. She escapes and returns to Holland to organize the war against the Burgundians. The struggle between Jacoba and the Burgundians involved as well a war between the nobility and the cities of Holland; the nobles (the "Hooks") sided with Jacoba and the cities (the "Codfish") with the Burgundian cause. Duke John IV of Brabant founded the University of Louvain.
1428	Jacoba is given back the titles and incomes from her lands, in return for which she acknowledges Philip the Good of Burdundy as her heir. Jacoba, however, secretly marries Frank van Borselen; Philip, fearing treachery, comes to Holland, imprisons Frank and forces Jacoba to renounce all claim to her lands. This means the incorporation of Holland and Zeeland and Hainaut into the Burgundian realm.
1429	Philip the Good takes definitive possession of the county of Namur.

1430   Philip the Good founds the Order of the Golden Fleece.

1435   Treaty of Arras between Philip the Good and Charles VII
                of France, a reversal of the Burgundian-English alliance.

1437   Revolt in Gent and Bruges against the authority of Philip
                the Good.

1438-41   War for the domination of the Baltic trade between Holland
                and Lubeck. The Baltic trade was to be the basis of
                Holland's trade system for centuries to come.

c. 1450   Decline of Bruges in Flanders as the Brabant towns of
                Antwerp and Bergen op Zoom attract more trade. The
                Hollanders manage to win predominance in the Baltic
                trade over the Hanseatic League.

1451   The death of Elizabeth of Gorlitz brings Luxemburg into
                the hands of Philip the Good of Burgundy.

1451-   Rebellion of Gent against the centralization brought about by
1453   Philip the Good. After its defeat, the city lost many of its
                privileges.

1464   The first meeting of the States General is held at Bruges
                in order to discuss the projected crusade of Philip the
                Good.

1465   Death of Philip the Bold, who is succeeded by his son,
                Charles the Bold. Of the present-day Netherlands, the
                east and northeast are still outside Burgundian possess-
                ions.

1468   Charles the Bold takes as his third wife, Margaretha of
                York, the sister of King Edward VI, thus entering into an
                alliance with England against France's Louis XI.

1469   Birth of Desiderius Erasmus of Rotterdam, who became
                famed as the leader of the humanist classical revival move-
                ment in northern Europe. He was responsible for the im-
                porting of many Renaissance ideals, as well as a critical
                attitude towards the Catholic Church, to France, the Low
                Countries and Germany, and preached a credo of toler-
                ation and intellectual freedom.

1473	Charles the Bold incorporates Guelders into the Burgundian realms. Charles and the German emperor, Frederick, discuss making Burgundy a kingdom, but the meeting has no results.
1474	At the inspiration of Louis XI of France, the League of Constance is formed to oppose Burgundy; Emperor Frederick of Germany and the Swiss cantons declare war on Burgundy.
1475	Charles the Bold conquers Lorraine.
1476	Charles the Bold was defeated by the Swiss at Granson and Murten.
1477	January 5. Charles the Bold was killed during the defeat of his army at Nancy in Lorraine.
	At the news of the death of Charles the Bold, many of his subserviant states attempted to win back their old rights. Louis XI of France occupied the duchy of Bourgogne and sends his armies north. Duchess Maria of Burgundy, 20, proclaims the constitution of the Grand Privilege on February 11, giving great powers to the Estates General and the provincial estates. In August Maria marries Maximilian of Habsburg. In the north, the Duchy of Guelders is reclaimed by its traditional dukes.
1482	Maria of Burgundy dies, leaving her three-year-old son, Philip the Fair, as Duke.
1483	Flanders institutes a Regency council for young Philip the Fair in order to further impair the authority of his father, Maximilian of Habsburg.
1483-1492	General rebellion in the Low Contries against the rule of the Burgundians. In 1483 there is an uprising in Flanders, crushed by Maximilian's mercenaries in 1485. Three years later Holland rebels unsuccessfully. A second Flemish rebellion in 1488, during which Maximilian is briefly imprisoned, also fails, as does a West Frisian uprising in 1491.

1492	Beheading of the Flemish rebel leader, Jan van Coppenhole, in Gent; the city surrenders to Maximilian, and the rebellion ends.

Charles of Egmond takes over the duchy of Guelders, freed from Burgundian rule. |
1493	Philip the Fair of Burgundy attains his majority.
1496	Philip the Fair marries Johanna, daughter of Ferdinand of Aragon and Isabella of Castile.
1498	An inconclusive campaign against Guelders is waged by Maximilian, while Albrecht of Saxony, the Stadholder of Philip the Fair, conquers Friesland. Groningen remains independent.
1500	Birth at Gent of the future Charles V, oldest son of Philip the Fair of Habsburg and Johanna of Aragon, who becomes heiress to the Spanish throne.
c.1500	Renaissance forms begin to penetrate the art of the Low Countries. Hieronymus Bosch, whose art was full of devils and hellfire, can be regarded as the last of the great medieval painters. Italian tendencies are visible in the Flemings Barend van Orly, Quenten Metsijs, Frans Floris and Jan Gossaert van Mabuse. Pieter Breughel the Elder (1525-1569) also employed Italian techniques. Artists of the Northern Netherlands typical of the Renaissance were Lucas van Leyden, Jan van Scorel, Maarten van Heemskert and Cornelis Engelbrechtsz.
1506	Sudden death in Spain of Philip the Fair.
1515	At the request of the nobility, Maximilian declares Charles V of age.
1516	Charles V becomes regent for his mother, Johanna, in Aragon and Castile upon the death of his grandfather, Ferdinand.
1519	Maximilian dies and Charles inherits Austria; he is elected German emperor. His position will involve the Netherlands in many European wars.

1523   The Lutheran Antwerpers Hendrik Voes and Jan van Essen
            are burned in Brussels, the first victims of Charles V's
            persecution of Protestantism.

1524   The province of Friesland recognizes Charles V as its
            lord.

1528   After some resistance, Charles V is recognized as the
            temporal lord of the bishopric of Utrecht. Charles, Duke
            of Guelders, names Charles V as heir to his lands.

1529   Peace of Kamerijk concluded between Charles V and
            Francis I of France. Francis gives up the town of
            Tournai as well as his suzerainty over Flanders and
            Artois.

1531   Reform of the central government by Charles, creating
            three councils to work with his governor of the Nether-
            lands: the Council of Finance, the Privy Council (for
            domestic affairs), and the Council of State, made up of
            the higher nobility.

            The organization of Anabaptist communities in the Neth-
            erlands by Melchior Hoffman. Large numbers of mainly
            lower-class people are attracted to this Protestant move-
            ment from Germany because of its communistic and pro-
            phetic elements.

1535   Unsuccessful attempt by the Anabaptists to take over
            Amsterdam, resulting in a wave of repression of Ana-
            baptism by the authorities.

            Pacifistic Mennonite movement organized by former
            priest, Menno Simonsz, in Friesland.

1536   Groningen recognizes Charles V as lord.

1539-   Great rebellion of Gent, at the end of which the city loses
1540   important privileges.

1543   Charles V concludes the Treaty of Venlo with Duke
            William of Guelders and Cleves accepting Charles as
            Duke of Guelders.

1548   Establishment of the "Burgundian Circle" at Augsburg by
         Charles V. The 17 units of the Low Countries (including
         Artois and Flanders) became a collective and inseparable
         part of the German Empire, with which it was to main-
         tain an essentially formal relationship.

1549   The "Pragmatic Sanction" enacted by the various provin-
         cial estates-general, proclaiming that the succession to
         Charles V would be uniformly accepted throughout the
         Netherlands.

1555   Charles abdicates in Brussels, disillusioned by his defeat
         in Germany by the German princes. He is succeeded as
         King of Spain and Lord of the Netherlands by his son,
         Philip II, who had grown up in Spain and was totally alien
         to the Low Countries.

1557   Resumption of war with France. Bankruptcy of Philip II,
         who is forced to convoke the States-General to ask for
         money.

1559   The papal bull "Super Universas" redivides the ecclesias-
         tical domains in the Netherlands in such a way that all the
         new dioces lie totally within the realms of Philip II and
         can thus more easily be controlled by him. The three
         archbishoprics are to be Utrecht, Mechelen and Cambrai,
         with fifteen suffragen bishoprics. Granvelle is appointed
         archbishop (later cardinal) of Mechelen. The nobility is
         now totally excluded from its former control of the epis-
         copal seats.

1561   William of Orange and the Count of Egmond protest that
         Philip's government relies too much on the King's Spanish
         advisors.

1561-   In Doornik and in other southern cities the singing of
1562   Protestant songs in the streets becomes common, as does
         Protestant sermon preaching in meadows and the freeing
         by force of Protestant prisoners. Incidents of iconoclasm
         occur at Valenciennes. The first Calvinist confession in
         the Netherlands, the "confessio Belgica" published.

1562   Formation of a league among the higher nobility consist-
         ing of Egmond, Orange, Hoorne, Hoogstraten, Bergen
         and Montigny. Montigny travels to Spain in order to
         bring the King the nobles' grievances (which consisted,

among other things, of objections to the new ecclesias-
tical divisions and to Cardinal Granvelle's excessive influence in the Netherlands' government, as well as to the
introduction of the Inquisition).

1564   Granvelle leaves the Netherlands for good. This repre-
        sents a temporary triumph for the high nobility.

1565   Egmond goes to Spain in a vain attempt to convince
        Philip II to relinquish some of his power in the Netherlands
        to the higher nobility. Philip, however, sends the famous
        "Letters from Segovia" to the Netherlands, confirming
        his arbitrary rule and urging stronger measures against
        the Protestants.

1565   December. Twenty noblemen form the "Compromis"
        league to combat the Inquisition. Four hundred other
        nobles soon join.

THE DUTCH REVOLUTION 1566-1609

1566   High wheat prices in 1565 create a revolutionary situation
        fomented by the opposition of the nobles and the exploitation
        of the religious issue. In April the league of the lower no-
        bility hand over their "Supplication" to the governess. In
        August riots break out everywhere. Several towns defy the
        government. On August 23, the governess Margaretha per-
        mits Protestant preaching. Some noblemen and towns rally
        to the government, fearing further popular uprisings.

1567   The Spanish government reconquers Tournai and Valen-
        ciennes. Orange, Brederode, Hoorne and Hoogstraten
        refuse to take the new oath to the King that Margaretha
        of Parma has requested of the nobility.

        May 24. The Spanish government issues a stern edict
        against the practice of Calvinism.

        August. Philip sends the feared Duke of Alva to the Neth-
        erlands to lead his troops, causing the flight of many
        rebels abroad. Some become pirates or guerrilla
        fighters in the Netherlands.

Establishment of the popularly known "Blood Council" by
Alva to suppress the rebels. Egmond and Hoorne are
arrested. The Council ultimately condemns 1100 to death,
and prosecutes 9,000.

1568   William of Orange raises a mercenary army and invades
the Netherlands, hoping to unleash a popular rebellion.
Hoorne and Egmond are executed in Brussels. Orange
withdraws and disbands his army in France because of
lack of funds.

1569   Alva tries to levy a punitive sales tax of 10% in the Netherlands, causing widespread protests.

1572   Third campaign of William of Orange, supported by the
French Huguenots in the south and the "Sea Beggars"
along the coast. Composition of the "Wilhelmus", the
Dutch national anthem, in honor of William's new campaign.

April. Sea Beggars conquer Den Briel, Flushing and
Veere.

May. Popular risings in favor of Orange in Holland and
Zeeland. Only Amsterdam, Middelburg and Goes do not
admit the Beggars.

July. The rebellious Holland cities meet in Dordrecht and
proclaim William Stadtholder.

August. St. Bartholomew's Eve in Paris, when the
Huguenots are exterminated by the French government;
this kills William's hope of French support and causes
his retreat.

December 15 - January 12, 1573. Siege of Haarlem.
After its fall to the Spanish, its garrison and many of
its citizens are beheaded.

1573   August 21 - October 8. Unsuccessful siege of Alkmaar
by the Spanish. Its defense is considered the beginning of
Dutch victory.

December. The practice of Catholicism is forbidden in
Holland.

1574	The Spanish are forced to give up the siege of Leiden.

1575   Establishment of the University of Leiden for the training of Reformed ministers.

1576   March 4. Death of the Spanish governor, Requesens. Since there is no one to succeed him, the Council of State takes over the government.

June. The Spanish conquer Zierikzee, but the unpaid troops mutiny and plunder their way through Brabant and Flanders.

September. In order to protect the land from the marauders, the Council of State summons the States General to Brussels, despite its ban by Philip II.

October. Representatives of the States General conclude the Pacification of Gent with the rebels of Holland and Zeeland: a new governor will be accepted only if he accepts the Pacification; the States General will determine the religious question; the edicts against heretics will be lifted; William of Orange will be the governor of Zeeland and Holland.

November. "The Spanish Fury" at Antwerp, when the mutinous Spanish soldiers plundered the (Spanish-ruled) city, killing 7,000 citizens, Spanish and Dutch alike.

The new Spanish governor of the Netherlands, Don Juan of Austria, bastard son of Charles V, arrives in disguise in the Netherlands.

1577   September. William of Orange is declared regent of Brabant. The States General name Archduke Mathias of Habsburg governor, but power remains in Orange's hands.

A wave of public indignation rises against Don Juan of Austria. Revolutionary governments are formed in Brussels and Antwerp in the following year and Calvinist governments are set up in all the cities of Flanders.

1578   January. A new, revolutionary Council of State is set up in Brussels, under Mathias and Orange.

February. Attempt of Orange to make a religious peace
fails; many cities, such as Amsterdam, Gent and Utrecht,
set up Protestant governments which forbid Catholicism.

Autumn. The Netherlands is now divided between four
governments: Spanish in the Southeast, Orange in Antwerp,
and in Brabant and Hainaut respectively the Calvinist.
John Casimir of the Palatinate and the Catholic nobility
(malcontents), who have come to the aid of their co-reli-
gionists.

October. Don Juan of Austria dies and the leadership of
the Spanish forces is taken over by Alexander Farnese,
Duke of Parma and son of Margaretha of Parma, former
governor of the Netherlands.

1579
January 6. The Union of Arras. Representatives of
Hainaut and the Estates of Artois form an alliance to pro-
tect Catholicism and support the King.

January 23. Guelders, Utrecht, Holland, Zeeland, most
of the southern cities and the Ommelanden sign the Union
of Utrecht, the most important points of which are:
1) The signees shall form an indivisible and eternal
   union.
2) Each province within the union shall maintain its
   unique laws, and will determine its own religion;
   no one, however, may be persecuted for the religion he practices.
3) None of the member provinces or cities may ally
   itself with another power, and none may secede
   from the union.

1580
March 15. Philip II offers 25,000 guilders, amnesty and
a peerage to anyone who will kill William of Orange.

1581
The States-General depose Philip II as Lord of the Netherlands.

1583
Prince William of Orange leaves Antwerp permanently
for Holland, settling first in the Hague and then in Delft.

1584
July 10. Balthasar Gerard murders William of Orange in
Delft. The States General decide to continue the struggle
for freedom and establish a Council of State of which

William's seventeen-year-old son, Prince Maurits, is a member, as well as representatives from Holland, Friesland, Brabant, Zeeland, Flanders, Utrecht and Mechelen.

1585   January. The Holy League is formed between Henry de Guise, the leader of the French Catholics, and Philip II. Henry III of France joins, thus refusing the offer of sovereignty made to him by the Northern Netherlands.

August. Parma conquers Brussels and Antwerp. He gives the Calvinists in his territories four years to either revert to Catholicism or emigrate. Many do emigrate to the north, some for purely economic reasons: Antwerp's position as a world trading center has been ended by the rebels' closing of the river Scheldt, whose access to the sea they have cut off.

Queen Elizabeth rejects an offer of sovereignty over the Northern Netherlands, but promises to send 5,000 troops under the command of a high English noble.

November. Prince Maurits of Orange elected Stadtholder in Holland and Zeeland.

December. Leicester lands in Flushing.

1585-   The first passage of a Dutch ship (the "White Lion", under
1586   the command of Steven van der Haghen) through the Straits of Gibraltar. By 1590 this passage was routine.

1586   February. Johan van Oldenbarnevelt appointed Grand Pensionary of Holland. He will dominate Dutch politics until his downfall in 1618, as an advocate of the provincial sovereignty of Holland and the supremacy of the state over the Calvinist Church.

1587   January. The English officers, Stanley and York, betray Deventer to the Spaniards; this compounds Dutch criticism of Leicester, who was also accused of destroying Dutch trade and of favoring the orthodox Calvinist party.

December. Leicester leaves the Netherlands for good; the command of the British troops is taken over by Willoughby.

1588   August. The English defeat the Spanish Armada in the
        Channel, with the support of a small number of ships from
        Zeeland. Parma is prevented from joining the Armada by
        the Dutch admiral, Justinus van Nassau.

1589   April. Mutineering English soldiers deliver the city of
        Geertruidenberg into the hands of Parma.

        August. Murder of King Henry III of France because of
        his dealings with the Protestants. Philip II claims the
        French throne for his daughter, Isabella, and orders
        Parma south to back up her claim, ignoring the fact that
        Parma is on the point of reconquering the Netherlands.

1590   March. Henry of Bourbon, the heir apparent to the
        French throne, defeats the army of the Catholic Holy
        League at Ivry. On March 4 there is a surprise attack on
        Breda by the forces of Prince Maurits aided by commandos
        hidden in a ship carrying peat.

        July. Parma's first French campaign.

        September. Maurits conquers Hemert, Crevecoeur,
        Hedel and Steenbergen.

1591   May - October. Prince Maurits reconquers Zutphen,
        Deventer, Delfzyl, Hulst and Nijmegen.

1592   July - September. Prince Maurits reconquers Steenwyck
        and Coevorden.

        December. Parma dies and Philip appoints Peter Ernest,
        Count of Mansfeld, as governor of the Netherlands.

1593   Return of Jan Huyghen van Linschoten to the Netherlands
        after many years in the Portuguese Indian service. His
        memoirs, Itinerario, become the guide for Dutch attacks
        on the Spanish-Portuguese empire in Asia.

1593-   Various expeditions to find a passage to India north of
1597   Russia, the most famous of which was that of 1596-7,
        when Heemskerck and Barentsz wintered on the island of
        Nova Zembla.

1594	Plancius and nine other Amsterdamers form a company with a capital of 300,000 guilders to finance voyages to India.
1595-1597	Pieter Keyzer commands the first Dutch expedition to the East Indies, which lands at Bantam in 1596.
1598	Spain concludes the peace of Vervins with Henry IV of France, in spite of Oldenbarnevelt's pleas to Henry. Philip II gives the entire Netherlands, including the North, which he no longer controls, to his daughter, Isabella, as dowry upon her marriage to Albert of Austria.
1598-1599	Second expedition to the Indies; this voyage commanded by Jacob van Neck, is a great financial success.
1598-1604	Olivier van Noort, commissioned by Rotterdam merchants, circumnavigates the globe, hoping in vain to capture some Spanish silver galleons.
1600	Prince Maurits undertakes a campaign in Flanders to free Flanders from Spanish domination and stop the Dunkirk pirates from their raids on Holland ships. Maurits beats the Spanish army at Niewpoort but the hoped-for uprising of the Flemish population against the Spanish does not take place, and Maurits withdraws. This is one of the last efforts by the Dutch to reconquer the Southern Netherlands.
1602	Founding of the Dutch East India Company. A commission of "17 Lords" is set up to manage the capital of 6-1/2 million guilders given out in shares. The Company is given a monopoly over all trade east of the Cape of Good Hope and with all lands reached through the Straits of Magellan. The Company is also given the power to maintain a war force, make treaties, and appoint governors and magistrates.
1605	The Portuguese are driven from the Moluccas and Steven van der Haghen establishes the power of the East India Company on the island of Amboina.
1606	The coast of Australia is reached for the first time by the Dutchman Willem Jansz. in his ship "Het Duyfken" (The Pidgeon).

1609   April 9. Twelve Year Truce signed in Antwerp, specifying that 1) Albert of Austria as well as Spain recognized
the sovereignty of the United Provinces; 2) both sides
were to keep the territories they then possessed.

Trading post established at Firando in Japan by the Dutch
East India Company.

Henry Hudson, commissioned by the Dutch East India
Company to find a northeast passage to the Indies, sails
in his ship, "The Half Moon", to the mouth of the Hudson,
which he names the "Mauritius" after Prince Maurits of
Nassau.

Founding of the "Wisselbank", a deposit and giro bank in
Amsterdam.

THE EMERGENCE OF THE DUTCH REPUBLIC (1609-1648)

1610   For several years a theological debate had been raging
between the professors Arminius and Gomarus of Leiden
University about the doctrine of predestination. Arminius
believed that all Christians could achieve salvation
through their own works and love of God; Gomarus held
the extreme Calvinist view that salvation was predes-
tined by God only for the elect. The theological problem
became political as the extreme Calvinist party also
wanted church supremacy over the state in certain
matters, and, furthermore, favored the war party. The
States of Holland and Utrecht tried to stop the theological
debate. In 1610 the "Remonstrance" was handed to the
States General by the Arminian, Uytenbogaert; the Armin-
ians were henceforth to be known as the Remonstrants,
and their opponents as Counter-Remonstrants, after
their Counter-Remonstrance of 1611.

1612   Treaty with the Sultan (in Istanbul), whereby Dutch trade
with Turkey is opened.

1614   Founding of the Northern Company to finance whaling expeditions. The Company was dissolved in 1642; only in
the second half of the 17th century did Dutch whaling become a significant operation.

1615-   Willem Schouten and Jacques Lemaire complete a voyage
1617   to the Indies around Cape Horn and the southern tip of
             Tierra del Fuego, but are imprisoned by Jan P. Coen,
             governor general of the East Indian Company.

1617   Riots in Den Briel, Haarlem, Rotterdam, Oudewater and
             the Hague against the Arminians. The lower classes, en-
             couraged by the ministers, sided with the Counter-Re-
             monstrants. Oldenbarnevelt and the Holland regents took
             the Arminian side because the Arminians felt that the
             government had the right to control the church.

             July 23. The Stadtholder, Prince Maurits of Orange,
             whose interests were consistently at odds with the power-
             ful Holland regents, chose the side of the Counter-Re-
             monstrants.

             August 4. At the behest of Oldenbarnevelt, the States of
             Holland adopt the "Sharp Resolution", in which they refuse
             to admit of a debate on the religious question, thus stress-
             ing the power of the state over the church. Oldenbarne-
             velt recommends that the cities augment their fighting
             forces, making the forces responsible to their city
             governments rather than to the Stadtholder. Maurits
             feels threatened by this development.

             November. In spite of the opposition of Utrecht, Holland
             and Overijssel, the States General decides for Maurits
             and orders a synod to be held to debate the religious ques-
             tion.

1618   July. Under pressure from Maurits, the States General
             decides to make Utrecht and Holland dismiss their pri-
             vate armies. Maurits goes to Utrecht for this purpose,
             while a delegation is sent by Holland to encourage Utrecht
             to hold out. Utrecht gives in to Maurits, who removes
             the Arminians from office in Utrecht and substitutes
             Counter-Remonstrants.

             November 13 - April 23, 1619. Synod of Dordrecht. The
             Arminians are expelled from the synod and the official
             doctrine of the church is proclaimed to be that of strict
             predestination. A decision is taken to sponsor a transla-
             tion of the Bible, which will ultimately result in the beauti-
             ful "Statenbijbel" (States Bible) of 1637.

1619   May. Execution of Oldenbarnevelt because of a) his en-
            couragement of the cities to build up their own armed
            forces and b) his encouragement of resistance. Hugo de
            Groot and Hogerbeets, allies of Oldenbarnevelt, are con-
            demned to life imprisonment.

            Governor General Coen builds the fortress of Batavia at
            the location of the settlement of Jacatra (now Djakarta).

1621   June 3. The Dutch West India Company is founded for
            purposes of trade with Africa and the West Indies; its
            administration is placed under the "Nineteen Lords". The
            Company's main aims are commerce, colonization, and
            attacks upon the Spanish Empire in America.

            Extermination of the inhabitants of the Banda Islands by
            Jan Pieterszoon Coen and Martinus Spronck in order to
            assure the undisturbed cultivation of nutmeg on the islands.

1623   Massacre of the English on the island of Amboina by the
            East India Company, which suspected the English of con-
            spiring against it.

1624   The Netherlands Republic concludes a treaty with France
            at Compiegne, whereby France promises financial help to
            the Netherlands in its war against Spain in return for which
            the Dutch will help Richelieu in his struggle against the
            Huguenots (French Protestants). In spite of their own
            Protestantism, the Dutch will later actually participate in
            the siege of the Huguenot harbor of La Rochelle.

1624-   The Dutch East India Company occupies Formosa, pre-
1642   viously Portuguese, and uses it as its headquarters for
            trade with China.

625   23 April. Upon the death of Prince Maurits, his brother,
            Prince Frederick Henry becomes the Stadholder of five of
            the seven provinces, while Groningen chooses the Frisian
            Stadtholder, Frederick's cousin, Ernst Casimir of Nassau.

            May. Breda surrenders to the Spanish general Spinola.

            Willem Verhulst buys the island of Manhattan from the
            Delaware Indians for sixty guilders. On the southern tip
            of the island, New Amsterdam is founded to serve as a

naval base for the territory of New Netherland, an area stretching from the Delaware River in the south to the Connecticut River in the north. At the time of the takeover by the British in 1664, the area contained around 10,000 Europeans, of which around 5,700 were Dutch.

1628   The Carribean islands of Tobago, Aruba, Bonaire and Curacao are occupied by the Dutch.

Piet Heyn captures the Spanish silver fleet, marking the only really successful undertaking of the Dutch West India Company.

1629   May 1. Princes Frederick Henry and Ernst Casimir begin the siege of Den Bosch, the beginning of a new drive to expel the Spanish from the Netherlands.

1632   Two generals in the Spanish service in the Southern Netherlands, Van den Bergh and Warfuse, come to the Hague with their plan to deliver part of the Spanish Netherlands into Dutch hands (the other half they plan to offer to France), on the condition that the practice of Catholicism be permitted. Venlo, Roermond and Maastricht are thus taken by the North. The expected popular uprising against the Spanish, however, fails to materialize.

1634-   Governship of Johan Maurits of Nassau in Brazil. During
1644   his tenure, Dutch authority in the territory was firmly established and considerable progress was made in the area. After he left, however, the Dutch regime there disintegrated rapidly.

1635   February. Treaty of partition between France and the Dutch Republic. The Spanish Netherlands is to be divided between France and the Republic roughly along the linguistic boundary. The Dutch and French armies unite to drive out the remaining Spanish, but receive no help from the populace.

1635-   Wild trading in tulip bulbs - just one aspect of the general
1637   lust for speculation indicative of the increasing wealth and prosperity of the Republic.

1637   Prince Frederick Henry reconquers Breda but loses Venlo and Roermond again to the Spanish.

1638- 1658	The Dutch East India Company captures the Portuguese forts on the island of Ceylon, a rich prize because of its wealth in cinnamon and rice.
1641	Prince William, the son and heir apparent of Prince Frederick Henry marries Mary Stuart, daughter of King Charles I of England. This marriage alliance was to be a divisive factor in Dutch politics because of the influence of foreign dynastic interest on Dutch diplomacy.

The Japanese permit Dutch traders to settle on the island of Decima in the harbor of Nagasaki, from which the Portuguese were driven two years previously. Until 1854 the Dutch on Decima were the only contact which the Japanese had with the outside world.

Malacca is conquered from the Portuguese.

1642	Abel Tasman begins his voyages in search of the Land of the South of which the ancient geographer Ptolemy speaks. In his travels he discovers Tasmania, the Fiji Islands, New Zealand and the Bismarck archipelago.
1645	The Republic sends an armed fleet through the Sont (the channel into the Baltic) without paying the customary toll to Denmark, thus demonstrating their sympathy with Sweden in the Swedish-Danish War.
1647	March 14. Prince Frederick Henry dies.
1648	January 30. Peace of Munster signed by Spain and the Republic. The most important points were:

1) Spain recognized the United Netherlands as a free and sovereign land.
2) Spain and the Netherlands should retain those territories of which they were then in possession, including those in the East and West Indies.
3) The Spanish would be excluded from those regions in the East and West Indies conquered by the Dutch.
4) The Scheldt and its corresponding sea-ways would continue to be closed by the States General.
5) The Catholics in the North would be allowed to practice their religion if they did so in a discreet manner.

THE DUTCH REPUBLIC AS A GREAT POWER (1648-1748)

1649   Charles I of England, the father-in-law of Stadtholder
                William II, is beheaded. William, who has great dynas-
                tic ambitions, calls for military intervention on behalf of
                the Stuarts. This leads to a confrontation with the peace
                party (the States of Holland, led by Amsterdam).

1650   June 4. Holland decides to disband part of the army.

                June 5. William II gets the States General to counteract
                the Holland order.

                June 6. Holland's representatives are arrested by
                William II.

                End of June. William Frederick, the Stadtholder's
                cousin, leads a sneak attack on Amsterdam, but the city
                is forewarned.

                August 3. Temporary truce between William and Amster-
                dam.

                November 6. William II dies of smallpox, leading to re-
                joicing amongst the peace party.

                November 14. Birth of William III.

1651   The "Great Meeting" in the Hague of deputies from the
                Provinces stresses the particular rights of the Provinces,
                which may appoint the officers of the troops which are in
                their pay, and decide on questions of religion.

                March. Proposal by England for a very close alliance
                with the Republic, which would mean war with France.
                The Republic declines.

                October. British Acts of Navigation, designed to push
                the Dutch out of trade with England.

1652   February. The States General decides to fit out 150 men
                o' war.

                May. Dutch Admiral Tromp refuses to salute the British,
                and this snub leads to the beginning of the First Anglo-
                Dutch war.

Jan van Riebeeck establishes a revictualing station at the Cape of Good Hope, intended partially to aid against scurvy.

1653   February. Dutch admiral Tromp loses the Three Day Sea Battle in the Channel to Blake, but manages to save his fleet. The British, now masters of the sea, capture many Dutch merchantmen.

Johan de Witt, born in 1625, becomes Grand Pensionary. De Witt was the leader of the Republican, anti-Orange party, which was in power until 1672.

"Pro-Orange Movements" spring up in various parts of the Netherlands during the first Anglo-Dutch War.

1654   Peace of Westminster between Britain and the Republic, specifying:
1) The Acts of Navigation remain in effect.
2) Dutch ships in English waters will be the first to strike the flag in salute.
3) Those guilty of the massacre of the British on Amboina shall be punished.
4) A secret and separate agreement providing that the States of Holland will nevermore elect a member of the House of Orange as their Stadtholder and will furthermore try to prevent an Orange being appointed Captain-General of the Republic.

Act of Seclusion, excluding the Oranges from office in Holland, passed in States of Holland in compliance with the Peace of Westminster. This act becomes the rallying point of Orangist opposition against the Republican party of De Witt.

1654-   Conquests of the Portuguese trading posts on Ceylon and
1658   along the coast of Malabar.

1656   During the war of Denmark and Poland against Sweden, and the consequent danger to shipping, the Dutch sent a fleet to protect their merchants in Danzig, a move symbolizing Dutch power in the Baltic, one of the mainsprings of their trade.

1658   Charles X of Sweden dictates the Peace of Roskilde to
            Denmark, giving Sweden control of the passage to the
            Baltic. Because of this threat to their trade interests,
            the Dutch ally with Denmark and defeat the Swedish fleet.

1659   Treaty of the Hague concluded by the Republic, France
            and England for the purpose of forcing Sweden to keep
            open the Oresund. Admiral de Ruyter sails with the
            Danes to enforce this resolution, which was done when
            De Ruyter defeated the Swedish admiral Nyborg at Funen.

1660   Restoration of the Stuarts in England and annulment of
            the Act of Seclusion barring the Oranges from the office
            of Captain-General.

1661   Peace with Portugal. Brazil is given up by the Dutch.

1662   Lukewarm treaty of friendship with England, which does
            nothing to clear up the points of conflict between the Dutch
            West India Co. and the English Africa Co.

            Offensive and defensive alliance between France and the
            Republic, but Grand Pensionary De Witt, who prefers not
            to have France as a near neighbor, rejects Louis XIV's
            offer to divide the Southern Netherlands along a line from
            Ostend to Maastricht.

1663   The States of Holland assume the guardianship of young
            William III of Orange. His Stuart-oriented tutor, Zuyle-
            stein, is dismissed, and Cpt. Buat, member of
            William's household, who has been conspiring to bring
            him to power through the help of the Stuarts, is con-
            demned to death, causing outrage among the Orangists.

1663-   A number of Dutch slave stations on the African coast are
1664   captured by Captain Holmes of the English Africa Company.

1664   English attacks without declaration of war on Dutch
            colonial holdings in America and Africa. Governor
            Pieter Stuyvsant surrenders New Amsterdam and New
            Netherland. De Ruyter reconquers the Republic's former
            African holdings.

            Colbert's policy of mercantilism introduces new high duty
            on goods imported into France in order to cripple Dutch
            trade.

1665-   Second Anglo-Dutch War.
1667

1665   March 4. Charles II of England declares war on the
             Republic.

             July 3. Sea battle off Lowestoft against the Duke of York,
             in which Van Wassenaar Obdam died and the Dutch were
             forced to withdraw.

             August. Bernard of Galen, bishop of Munster, paid large
             sums by the British, invades the Republic from the East.

1666   Bishop of Munster signs peace treaty at Cleves.

             June. De Ruyter defeats the fleets of the English admiral
             Monk and of Rupert of the Palatinate at North Foreland.

1667   Abraham Crijnssen conquers Surinam, which is con-
             firmed by the Peace of Breda as a possession of the States
             of Zeeland.

             Maccassar (in the East Indies) conquered by Cornelis
             Speelman, who secures a trade monopoly for the Dutch
             East India Company.

             The States of Holland adopt the "Eternal Edict" whereby
             Holland abolishes the provincial Stadtholdership. This
             edict represents a triumph for the anti-Orange party.

             June. De Ruyter and Cornelis De Witt are commissioned
             by the States General to sail to the mouth of the Thames.
             The Dutch break the defensive chain across the Thames
             at Medway and sail right up to Chatham, there they des-
             troy much of the English fleet; they take as prize the
             English flagship "Royal Charles". Panic prevails in
             London, where an immediate attack is feared.

             July. The Peace of Breda is hastily concluded between
             the British and the Dutch, whereby
             1) Each power retains its present possessions, con-
                firming the Dutch loss of New Amsterdam and its
                possession of Surinam.
             2) The Acts of Navigation shall not pertain to products
                coming to England via the Scheldt and the Rhine.

3) The principle of "free ship - free goods" is accepted. Dutch ships shall not be searched, only their papers inspected and only war material will be regarded as contraband.

1667-
1668

The War of Devolution between Spain and France for the conquest of the Southern Netherlands. For the Republic, which wants a buffer between France and itself, this war endangers the relation with the French ally.

1668

January. Triple Alliance between England, Sweden and the Republic, for the purpose of maintaining the peace between Spain and France, by force, if necessary.

May. Peace of Aix-la-Chapelle. Louis XIV is forced to give up his plans for the conquest of the Southern Netherlands, keeping only the little territory that he had already occupied. Louis blames the Republic for this defeat.

1670

Secret treaty of Dover concluded between Louis XIV and Charles II of England, with the following terms:
1) Mutual support is promised in the event of an attack on the Southern Netherlands or the Republic, and
2) England will receive Walcheren and the Scheldt delta.

1671

December. Mutual defense alliance between the Republic and Spain for the event of a French attack.

Louis XIV concludes treaties with the bishops of Munster and Cologne against the Republic.

1672

February. Under the pressure of the tense international situation, William III of Orange appointed Captain-General.

March. England declares war on the Republic.

April. France, Munster and Cologne declare war on the Republic.

June 7. De Ruyter beats the English and French fleets at Solebay, England.
June 9. Groningen besieged by Bishop of Munster, who is forced to withdraw in August.

June 12. French army crosses the Rhine and William III
withdraws behind the waterline.
June 21. Fall of Utrecht and dispatch by Louis XIV of
punitive peace terms to the States General. Four
Orangists make an attempt on the life of De Witt, who is
critically wounded. The Republic's situation seems hope-
less.

July 2. The States of the various provinces name
William III as Stadtholder.
July 3. The States General name William Captain-
General. William III and the States General refuse to
accept the French surrender terms and swiftly strengthen
the Dutch army. Louis XIV returns to France, leaving
his army under the command of Luxemburg.

August. Attempted English landing at Kijkduin foiled by
De Ruyter.

September. Troops of Dutch ally Emperor Leopold of
Germany force French troops to withdraw to defend their
southern flank.

December. William III pushes south, relieving Maastricht. Luxemburg manages to cross the frozen water
line into Holland, but must withdraw with the thaw.

1673   November. The English parliament refuses to vote
Charles II more money for the war.

December. William III captures Bonn, the French ar-
senal and forces the French troops to leave the Northern
Netherlands.

1674   February 19. Second Peace of Westminster between
England and the Republic, reestablishing pre-war condi-
tions (New Netherland, which had been retaken by the
Dutch in 1673, was restored to England).

Liquidation of the original Dutch West India Company and
establishment of another with less capital and fewer
directors.

1675	William III becomes hereditary Stadtholder for Holland and Zeeland. The States General make the Captain-Generalship hereditary for William III.
1676	The Dutch fleet under De Ruyter engages the French fleet in the Mediterranean, scoring victories at Stromboli and Etna, where De Ruyter is killed, but suffering defeat at Palermo.
	Peace negotiations with the French begin at Nijmegen.
1677	Marriage of William III with Mary Stuart, niece of Charles II and second in line for the English throne.
1678	Defensive alliance of the Republic with England.

1678 — August 10. Separate peace with France concluded at Nijmegen, since the Estates of Holland refuses to grant more money for the war to William III, who is violently opposed to peace. The other allies, the Emperor and the Spanish, are forced by the Dutch action to concluded unfavorable peaces with France and regard the Dutch as traitors. The terms are:
   1) The Dutch get back all territory occupied by the French.
   2) The high French import tax of 1667 will no longer be imposed on Dutch goods.

1681	Four-way treaty between the Republic, Spain, Sweden and the Emperor for the purpose of maintaining the Peaces of Nijmegen and Munster.
1683	Spain declares war on France because the latter has attacked the Southern Netherlands. The Republic sends troops to aid Spain on the basis of the alliance of 1681; a conflict arises between William III who wants to give strong support and Amsterdam which wishes to avoid the conflict.
1685	Revocation of the Edict of Nantes in France, meaning that the Huguenots were no longer free to practice their religion; as a result, many thousands were to leave for the Netherlands, Switzerland, England and even South Africa, taking their trading abilities and connections with them.

The Catholic James II, William III's father-in-law, becomes King of England.

1686   The Alliance of Augsburg is concluded between Spain, the
            Emperor of Germany, Sweden and various smaller
            German states against France.

1688   Anti-royalist and anti-French party in England ask
            William III and his wife to intervene.

            June 10. James II has a son, whom William and Mary
            claim to be a baby substituted for the real, stillborn,
            heir. The son, and not William and Mary, becomes the
            heir to England.

            November. William lands in England with the per-
            mission of the States General with the purpose of
            "restoring the laws and freedoms of the English". The
            parliament party and part of the English army join
            William. James II flees to France and Louis XIV immed-
            iately declares war on the Republic, although he pretends
            it is for other reason than William's expedition. This is
            the beginning of the Nine Years War (1688-1697).

1689   English parliament declares William and Mary King and
            Queen (William had refused to be simply consort).

            May. Great Alliance of Vienna between the Emperor and
            the Republic, joined by England, Brandeburg, and (in
            1690) Spain. This was William III's long-dreamed of
            great league against France. Its purpose was to bar
            Louis XIV and his family from the Spanish succession
            after the expected death of Charles II of Spain.

1690   In Ireland William defeats James II, forcing him off the
            island in 1691 (William is still a hero to the Protestants
            of Northern Ireland, who call themselves "Orangemen"
            to this day).

1695   Death of Queen Mary of England, weakening her hus-
            band's position.

            Bombardment of Brussels by the French, destroying the
            Grand Place.

Introduction to Java from Arabia of the cultivation of coffee.

1697   September 20. Peace of Ryswyck between the allies (England, the Republic, Spain and the Emperor) and France, the terms of which largely confirmed the status quo.

1697-   Czar Peter the Great of Russia visits Zaandam and Am-
1698   sterdam, where he works for some time in a shipyard.

1698   First Partition Treaty (at the Hague) of the Spanish in-heritance made by England, the Republic and France. While Louis XIV on the one hand wants a Bourbon on the Spanish throne, and the sea powers on the other hand have agreed on a Habsburg (Emperor Leopold of Austria), the signers finally agree on Joseph Ferdinand, the six-year-old son of Maximilian Emanuel II of Bavaria, the governor of the Southern Netherlands.

1700   The death of Joseph Ferdinand of Bavaria (1699) necessi-tates the Second Partition Treaty between England, the Republic and France; Charles of Austria is to receive the entire Spanish inheritance. Louis XIV wants the King of Bavaria to rule the Southern Netherlands.

               Death of Charles II of Spain, whose will names Philip of Anjou, Louis' grandson, heir to all Spanish possess-ions. In spite of all previous agreements, Louis decides to support Philip, who is now hailed as King of Spain.

               Philip of Anjou refuses to give up his future claims to the French throne and proceeds to grant France wide econ-omic privileges.

1701   King Maximilian Emanuel of Bavaria chooses the side of France. Louis XIV occupies the Southern Netherlands, producing great anti-French sentiment in the Republic and England.

               September 7. Alliance of the Hague between England, the Republic, and the Austrian emperor. Spanish possessions in the Netherlands and Italy were to be given to Austria; England and the Netherlands would have a free hand in the conquest of the Spanish colonies.

1702   March 19. Death of William III.

              May. Declaration of war on France by England and the
              Republic (War of the Spanish Succession).

1702-   Second Stadtholderless Period. Taking advantage of the
1747   childlessness of William III, Holland and most of the
              other provinces decide not to appoint another Stadtholder.

1706   Marlborough is victorious at Ramillies in the Southern
              Netherlands, as a result of which Flanders and Brabant
              recognize Charles of Austria as their sovereign.

1709   Battle of Malplaquet between the allies and France results
              in loss of thousands on both sides.

1711   Death of Emperor Joseph I of Austria; his brother,
              Charles, the designated successor in Spain, now inherits
              Austria as well, which presents the danger of Habsburg
              supremacy. Britain and France begin peace negotiations,
              in which Dutch considerations are completely ignored.
              The decline of the Republic as a great power is now ob-
              vious.

1713   Peace of Utrecht between England, the Republic, Prussia,
              Portugal and Savoy on the one hand, and France on the
              other. The principal terms were:
                1) Philip of Anjou gets the Spanish throne and colonies,
                   but renounces his claim to France.

                2) Spanish Italy and the Southern Netherlands are given
                   to Austria.

                3) The Republic gets part of present day northern Lim-
                   burg, Prussia another.

                4) The princedom of Orange (present-day Orange in
                   France) becomes definitively French.

                5) The Southern Netherlands remains under an Anglo-
                   Dutch condominium until definite border arrange-
                   ments are made with Austria.

1715   Border agreement between Austria, the Republic and
              England:

1) The Republic has the right to garrison its troops in many Southern Netherlands cities (mainly Flemish) along with Austrian troops.

2) The Scheldt is to remain closed and trade to the Indies is forbidden the Southern Netherlands.

3) England and the Republic will receive favorable import privileges in the Southern Netherlands.

1716-1717	Great Meeting of the States General of the Republic for the purpose of reforming the revenue system (The Republic was near bankruptcy, in spite of the great wealth still in the land). No results are forthcoming.
1721-1722	Jacob Roggeveen commissioned by the West India Company to make a voyage to the "Southland", in the course of which he discovers Easter Island.
1729	William IV, grand-nephew of William III, reaches his majority and assumes the Stadtholdership of Friesland and Groningen, Drenthe and Gelderland.
1734	William IV marries Anne, the daughter of King George III of England.
1747	April 24. Because of the invasion of Zeeland Flanders by the French, the masses begin a movement in favor of the leadership of Orange. April 28. Zeeland proclaims William IV Stadtholder and Captain-General. May. All the other provinces proclaim William IV Stadtholder. December. William IV recognized as hereditary Stadtholder.
1748	William IV is asked to make widespread reforms in prevailing official corruption; specifically it is asked that he prevent the sale of offices, that he assign postal revenue to the state, and that he restore guild privileges.

1749   Third War of the Javanese Succession, resulting in the
                partition of Mataram into the states of Djokjakarta and
                Surakarta.

THE DECLINE OF THE REPUBLIC AND THE PERIOD OF DEMOCRATIC REVOLUTION AND FRENCH OCCUPATION (1748-1813)

1751   Death of William IV.

1751-   Regency of William V's mother Anne for her young son.
1759

1756-   Seven Years' War between Austria, France, England and
1763   Prussia; the Republic remains neutral, in spite of
                England's expectations, if only because of its general
                military weakness. Many of its ships and their cargoes
                are confiscated by the British.

1759   Attempt to restore Dutch authority in Bengal squelched
                by Lord Clive.

1763   The end of the Seven Years War brings about a crisis on
                the Amsterdam stock exchange.

1764   Climax in the controversy between the proponents of the
                expansion of the army and the restoration of the fleet,
                and their opponents. Amsterdam blocks all progress by
                refusing to agree to an army expansion without there
                being an agreement on sharing the annual cost of supply-
                ing the fleet.

1775   The army and navy struggle becomes a prestige question
                between William V (and his field marshal Brunswick), and
                Amsterdam. It becomes more important because of the
                impending war between England and her American colo-
                nies.

                St. Eustatius, a Dutch island in the Caribbean, blossoms
                as a harbor for trading contraband from Europe with the
                rebellious American colonies. The island becomes known
                as the "Golden Rock".

1777   Agreement finally arrived at to equip twenty men o' war
                for about fourteen months.

1778	France declares war on England.
	Amsterdam refuses to abide by British contraband rules. Amsterdam and the Americans discuss the possibility of a trade agreement at Aix-la-Chapelle.
1779	On the grounds of the defensive alliance of 1678 England asks the Republic for help against Spain and France.
	John Paul Jones is given a hero's welcome in the Republic, while England demands his extradition.
1780	The outline of the Dutch-American treaty of Aix-la-Chapelle falls into English hands.
	December 10. The Republic signs an agreement of armed neutrality with Catherine of Russia and other powers.
	December 20. England declares war on the Dutch.
1780-1784	Fourth Anglo-Dutch War, in which the Netherlands fleet, badly outnumbered by the 122 British ships of the line, suffers catastrophically. The Patriots, members of the party for democratic reform, blame William V and the Orangists.
1781	August 5. Battle at Doggersbank, when a Dutch armed convoy manages to escape destruction by the British.
	September 26. Publication of the Patriot Party's pamphlet "To the Dutch People", advocating democratic reforms.
1782	Growth of the Patriot Party, which draws up a program and organizes militias.
	The States General decide on an entente with France and recognition of American independence.
1784	Peace of Paris with England, whereby the Republic gives up Negapatnam and gives the British free passage in the Moluccan Islands.
	December. Meeting of all the volunteer corps in Utrecht to discuss the establishment of a new (democratic) constitution.

1785   Defensive alliance of the Republic with France.

1786   August. William V is encouraged to act more aggressively against the Patriots by his brother-in-law Frederick William II, the new king of Prussia. He sends his troops to occupy Patriot-oriented towns. Holland defends its borders against the prince by a cordon of volunteer corps.

1787   June 28. Princess Wilhelmina, wife of William V, is arrested by a volunteer Patriot corps and she appeals for help to her brother, King Frederick William II of Prussia.

September 13. Ferdinand of Brunswick meets little resistance in his invasion of the Republic.

September 18. The States of Holland annul all their pronouncements against William's authority.

October 10. Amsterdam surrenders to Prussian troops and many Patriots flee for France, which has, however, failed to send aid against Prussia.

1788   All regents must swear an oath of allegiance to the existing government.

April. Defensive alliance with England and Prussia.

1791   West India Company dissolved when its charter is not renewed.

1793   February 1. France, whose monarchy has been replaced by a democratic republic, declares war on England and on the Republic.

1795   January 18. France occupies the Republic, but before it invades Amsterdam, Schimmelpenninck takes over the city government in the name of the revolutionary "Provisional Government". William V flees to England.

16 May. Treaty of the Hague between France and the Republic, stipulating
   1) A defensive and offensive alliance between France and the Netherlands.

2) The Republic must send half of its fleet and army to the aid of France and must feed and clothe 25,000 French troops.

3) Zeeland Flanders, Maastricht and Venlo would be annexed by France.

4) France would receive 100 million guilders for damages.

England declares war because of this treaty and begins its occupation of Dutch colonies.

1796   March. First meeting of the National Assembly, which immediately proclaims the division of church and state, extends equal citizenship to the Jews and draws up a moderate confederalist constitution. The battle about centralization or provincial state-rights becomes the big issue.

1797   August 1. First meeting of the Second National Assembly, which is more radical than the First National Assembly.

1798   January 22. Radical coup d'etat led by Wybo Fynje and Pieter Vreede. 22 Federalists in the National Assembly are imprisoned and the other delegates are required to take an oath rejecting the authority of the Stadtholder, aristocracy and provincial state rights.

April. Outline for the new constitution promulgated, whereby it is proposed
1) a representative body elected by a broad franchise, with legislative (including fiscal) powers
2) an executive council, named by the representatives
3) The country is to be divided into 8 departments which in no way correspond to the traditional provinces. Department and local authorities are also to be elected by the citizens. The guilds are to be disbanded.

June 12. Coup d'etat of the moderates, led by Daendels, in order to force the instrumentation of the new constitution; the radicals now seem more prone to establish a sort of dictatorship instead.

July. Regular elections held under the Constitution of 1798.

1801	September. Coup d'etat led by General Augereau, commander of French forces in the Netherlands, and three members of the executive council; in keeping with the new developments in France at this time, Augereau's group introduces a conservative government.
1802	Peace of Amiens with England; the Republic gets her colonies back from England, with the exception of Ceylon.
1803	War with England breaks out again and once more the Republic loses her colonies.
1805	A new constitution is dictated by Emperor Napoleon, who wants more Dutch support against England. A Grand Pensionary becomes chief executive, exercising many sovereign powers, for a term of 5 years. Schimmelpenninck is the first Grand Pensionary named. The legislature, a group of 19, is to be named by the Grand Pensionary (later by the department governments).
1806	The new government makes wide reforms, such as passing the compulsory school law, establishing a system of public schools, and making new laws regulating the postal system, spelling and medical education. Death of William V. Napoleon makes his brother King of the Netherlands because he wants to make Holland part of his "Continental System". November. Decree of Berlin establishes the Continental System, to which Holland is now forced to belong.
1810	July 9. The Kingdom of Holland is incorporated into France by the Decree of Rambouillet. Charles-Francois Lebrun becomes governor and Amsterdam is made third capital of the Empire. The Dutch language is maintained as official language along with French.
1811	The last remaining Dutch colony, Java, falls to the British, who rule there until 1816.
1812	Napoleon's march to Russia. Around 15,000 Dutch draftees were in the campaign.

LIBERATION AND ESTABLISHMENT OF THE
KINGDOM OF THE NETHERLANDS (1813-1848)

1813   After the defeat of Napoleon at Leipzig, French troops
begin to withdraw from the Netherlands.

November 15. Falck establishes a provisional government at Amsterdam.

November 20. Direction of the government is taken over
by Van der Duyn, Van Maasdam and Van Hogendorp.

December 2. Installation of the prince of Orange as
sovereign in Amsterdam, which was proclaimed capital.
The prince guarantees a free constitution.

1814   March 29. A new constitution is promulgated, providing:
1) The sovereign prince is the chief executive and is
   solely responsible for the colonies. He must belong
   to the Reformed Church.

2) A legislature is chosen by the provincial States. It
   has only limited budgetary powers.

3) The ministers are responsible only to the king.

4) The provincial States are chosen by three groups:
   the nobles, the representatives of the cities and
   the representatives of the rural areas.

July 21. The Eight Articles of London provide for the
unification of Belgium and the Netherlands. There will
be freedom of religion and Belgium will be represented
in the States General.

August 1. William I becomes sovereign of Belgium.

Establishment of the Bank of the Netherlands, chartered
to issue currency.

Agreement with England concerning the return of the
occupied Dutch colonies (except the Cape Colony, Ceylon,
Demerary, Essequibo and Berbice).

1815　　　April. A new constitution is promulgated, providing for
an upper house of distinguished men appointed by the
king, and a lower house, having the right of initiating
legislature, chosen by the provincial States and consisting of 55 members from Belgium and 55 from the Netherlands (although Belgium was more heavily populated).
The legislature would sit alternatively in Brussels and
the Hague and it would no longer be obligatory for the
King to be a member of the Reformed Church. The uni-
fied country consisted of 17 provinces. William I proclaimed King.

June. Defeat of Napoleon, who had escaped from Elba in
March, at the Battle of Waterloo, in Belgium. Crown
Prince William played a role in the fighting.

September. The Bishop of Gent forbids Catholics to take
the oath of allegiance. The other Catholic bishops concur in this and many Catholic officials resign.

1816　　　Reorganization of the Dutch Reformed Church, giving the
government greater powers.

Protective tariff established, intended to favor Belgian
industry.

Restoration of Dutch rule over Surinam and the Dutch
Antilles. The slave trade remains forbidden there.

1819　　　New language law providing that hereafter only the Dutch
language could serve as the official language in the Dutch
speaking part of the Southern Netherlands (Belgium).

1822 and　New laws governing religiously-sponsored educational
1824　　　institutions, providing that all such schools must obtain
a license. In practice this gave a monopoly to state
secondary and elementary schools.

1823　　　G. M. Roentgen, an improver of the steam engine, establishes the Dutch Steamboat Company, with its base at
Feyenoord (Rotterdam).

1824　　　Establishment of the Dutch Trading Company, designed to
win back a prominent place in world commerce for the
Dutch. The King himself is a major stockholder.

Treaty between England and the Netherlands, admitting England to trade with the Dutch East Indies. The Dutch recognize England's sovereignity over Malacca and Singapore, but England gives up all claims to Sumatra.

1825   Establishment of state-run "Philosophical College" in Louvain, which all Roman Catholic student priests were obliged to attend.

1825-
1830   The Java War. The resistance of the Javanese nobility, led by Diponegoro, to Dutch encroachments and restrictions, was crushed and its leaders imprisoned.

1827   Concordat with the Pope ending the monopoly of the Philosophical College.

1828   Alliance between the liberals and Catholics to redress the religious injustices and demand constitutional reform. Widespread movements petitioning the King.

1829   The lower house rejects the budget as a gesture of protest against the King.

1830   August 25. After the success of the July revolution in France, there are riots and attacks in Brussels on the house of the Minister of Justice. The proletariat joins, made more rebellious by the year's industrial crisis. Plundering continues until August 27, when a civilian militia is established by the upper class to preserve order. Riots also occur in other cities, including Lieges.

September 1. Representatives of the States General meet with the king in Brussels and convince him that peace can be assured by an administrative division of the united lands.

September 5. The king asks the States General to decide either to annul the constitution or to create an administrative division.

September 23 - 26. Prince Frederick of Orange is forced by street fighting to give up his attempt to occupy Brussels.

End of September. The States General vote for separate administration of the two countries, but this comes too late, as the Dutch by this time have been completely driven out of Belgium.

October. The Crown Prince tries unsuccessfully to make himself the leader of the Belgian independence movement.

November 4. Meeting of the great powers at London. A cease fire is proclaimed.

November 10. Gathering of a National Congress at Brussels, chosen by popular election.

November 18. National Congress proclaims Belgium independent and bars the House of Orange from the Belgian throne in perpetuity.

General van den Bosch imposes the "culture system" on Indonesia, stipulating that one-fifth of the land must be cultivated with commercially valuable products such as coffee and sugar. The population is thus subjected to the arbitrary rule of local colonial officials.

1831 January. The conference of great powers in London issues the "January Protocols", regulating the separation of Belgium and the Netherlands. The provisions are accepted by William I but rejected by the Belgian National Congress, since the Netherlands is allowed to maintain its 1790 borders, and receives Luxemburg as well. Moreover, 16/31 of the Dutch national debt is levied on Belgium.

February 7. Proclamation of the Belgian constitution, establishing a constitutional monarchy, with an aristocratic upper house and a lower house of representatives. The ministers are to be responsible to the parliament and not to the king, as in the Netherlands.

June. Leopold of Saxe-Coburg chosen as King of Belgium. He accepts only after the controversy over the January Protocols has been settled in Belgium's favor. William I rejects the new settlement.

August 2 - August 12. Ten day campaign of the Dutch
army against Belgium. The Dutch defeat the Belgians at
Hasselt and Louvain, but must retreat before the French
army.

1833   May 21. London convention between England, France
and the Netherlands, resulting in a cease-fire and the
maintenance of the status quo, meaning that Belgium
kept Limburg and Luxemburg and that England and
France lift their embargos and blockades.

1833-   In order to spread their authority over Padang and
1837   Minangkabause, the Dutch go to war with the padri's,
an Islamic sect on Sumatra.

1834   Secession from the established Reformed Church led by
De Cock of Ulrum and Scholte of Doeveren, who advo-
cated stricter, more Fundamentalist religious practice.
The government undertakes measures against the seced-
ers.

1837   Appearance of the Arnhemse Courant as the first
clearly liberal newspaper in the Netherlands.

Potgieter founds De Gids, a critical literary journal with
a liberal slant.

1839   Final treaty with Belgium, whereby

1) Limburg and Luxemburg will be partitioned.
   William I remains Grand Duke of the Duchy of
   Luxemburg.

2) Dutch Limburg and the duchy of Luxemburg become
   members of the German League.

3) Belgium shall be neutral in perpetuity, and its
   neutrality shall be guaranteed by the great powers.

4) Belgium shall pay 5 million guilders annually towards the Dutch national debt.

Opening of the first Dutch railroad between Haarlem and
Amsterdam.

THE ESTABLISHMENT OF PARLIAMENTARY MONARCHY
(1840-1868)

1840   Constitutional reform necessitated by the separation
from Belgium. Attempts at liberalization fail. The king
is forced to abdicate in favor of his son because of popular displeasure at his planned marriage with the Belgian
Catholic countess Henriette d'Oultremont.

1841   National bankruptcy avoided only by arbitrary liquidation
of the deferred national debt.

       The seceders of 1834 are officially recognized, but many
nevertheless subsequently emigrate to America, where
they settle principally in Michigan and Iowa.

1842   The established Reform Church is freed of state supervision.

1844   The "Proposition of the Nine Men" put forth by a group of
nine liberals led by Thorbecke and Luzac for liberalization of the constitution. It is not taken up in parliament
as the prevailing sentiment is that such measures must
be initiated by the king.

1845   Failure of the potato crop leads to the introduction of
free trade in grain.

1847   Riots in protest against unemployment and the high cost
of food.

1848   February. Revolution in Paris sparked democratic revo-
lutions all over Europe.

       March. Riots in the Hague and Amsterdam, and the
temporary success of the revolution in Prussia, make
a fearful William II consider liberal constitutional reforms.

       March 17. Formation of a royal commission for con-
stitutional reform, led by Thorbecke, who emerges as
the great liberal leader.

       November 3. Promulgation of the new constitution, the
most important provisions of which were

1) The lower house is to be directly elected by popular vote and is to have the rights of amendment, interpellation and investigation. The franchise is still restricted.

2) The upper house is to be chosen by the provincial states from among the most highly taxed people in the country.

3) All meetings of the representative bodies must be public.

4) The ministers are to be responsible to parliament.

5) Freedom of education, assembly, press, opinion and religion.

Constitutional reform removes the right of personal rule over the colonies from the king.

1849   Death of King William II, who is succeeded by his son, William III.

Formation of the first Thorbecke cabinet, made difficult because of the personal and ideological antipathy of the new king for Thorbecke.

1853   March. Restoration of a Catholic episcopal hierarchy in the Netherlands: establishment of 5 bishoprics, at Utrecht, Haarlem, Shertogenbosch, Roermond and Breda. Thorbecke's refusal to prevent this causes resentment among Protestants, who organize the April Movement. The king's unconstitutional support for the Protestants causes Thorbecke's resignation.

1857   Passage of Van Rappard's school law, providing free elementary education but forbidding sectarian religious instruction in the state schools.

1859   Prohibition of slavery in the Dutch East Indies.

1860   Passage of Van Hall's Railroad Bill, providing for the construction of railroads by the state, but for their management by private companies: Subsequent rapid expansion of the rail network stimulates the economy.

Max Havelaar, by the Dutch author, Multatuli, appears, drawing attention to the exploitation and injustice of the "culture system" in the Netherlands Indies.

1863   Prohibition of slavery in the Dutch West Indies.

1866-   Minority government of Van Zuylen van Nijevelt, during
1868   which the controversy is resolved over whether a minis-
              ter with the king's support may retain office against the
              wish of the majority.

1867   February. Rumors about negotiations between William III
              and Emperor Napoleon III of France over the sale of
              Luxemburg (of which the king was Grand Duke). Bismarck,
              fearing French encroachments, turns this into an inter-
              national crisis. A London conference takes up the ques-
              tion.

              May 11. Luxemburg and Limburg leave the German League.
              The Netherlands and the great powers guarantee the neu-
              trality of Luxemburg.

THE GROWTH OF THE MODERN PARTY-STATE,
ECONOMIC REVIVAL (1868-1914)

1868   Pastoral letter from the Dutch Catholic bishops rejecting
              the religiously neutral state school system; this marked
              the beginning of the gradually deepening schism between
              the Catholics and the liberals, and the beginning of the
              battle for parochial schools. This question is the basis
              for a new party alignment of religious (Protestant as well
              as Catholic) parties against non-religious (liberals and,
              later, socialists).

1869   Opening of the Suez Canal, bringing the East Indies much
              closer to the Netherlands and therefore, much more
              attractive for investment.

1870   Aletta Jacobs is permitted to attend the state high school
              in Sappemeer, thus beginning the female emancipation
              movement in the Netherlands.

              Abolution of capital punishment.

              The "culture system" of governmentally forced production
              of agricultural products in Indonesia is ended in principle

by Minister of Colonies De Waal, who also makes it possible for individuals to lease government land in the Indies.

1871- 1872	Third Thorbecke cabinet, with a mandate to reform the army. Thorbecke died in 1872.
1872	End of the prohibition of trade unions, and consequent legalization of strikes. Opening of the "New Waterway", the canal linking Rotterdam with the sea, the beginning of Rotterdam's rapid rise to the position of the first harbor of the Dutch empire.
1873- 1904	Atjeh War, a costly campaign to conquer Atjeh (Sumatra); the war drags on interminably due to die-hard resistance of the population.
1878	Elementary School Bill of Kappeyne van de Coppello leads to improvement in instruction but maintains the state's refusal to subsidize religious education. The orthodox Calvinists (the Anti-Revolutionary Party) and the Catholics, both of which groups want to establish their own school systems with a state subsidy, are driven into an alliance. Establishment by Abraham Kuyper of the rigidly Calvinist Anti-Revolutionary Party, the first tightly organized political party in the Netherlands.
1880	Foundation of the Free University of Amsterdam by the orthodox Calvinists, led by Abraham Kuyper. August 31. Birth of the future queen, Wilhelmina.
1881	Establishment of the Social-Democratic League by H. Gerhardt and F. Domela Nieuwenhuis.
1887	Constitutional Reform. The amount of tax payments are no longer to be the basis for determining the franchise. The tax criterion is now combined with the criterion of mental capability and social standing. The lower house is to consist of one hundred members, changing every four years. The upper house is to have fifty members; eligibility is now widened to include those who have held high office.

1888	First election held according to the constitutional reforms of 1887. The electorate has been broadened from 100,000 to around 300,000. A right wing majority is created; Domela Niewenhuis elected the first Socialist in parliament. The rightist Mackay cabinet is formed.
1889	Elementary school bill grants the same subsidy to religious schools that it gives regular state schools. Ruys de Beerenbrouck Labor Bill forbidding child labor and regulating the labor of women and young people.
1890	Death of King William III. Queen Emma is regent for her ten-year-old daughter, Wilhelmina. Establishment of Royal Dutch Petroleum.
1892	Abraham Kuyper's group of orthodox Calvinists separates from the Reformed Church, deploring its laxness. The group calls itself the Gereformeerd (meaning original, or orthodox, Reformed).
1892-1893	Minister Pierson passes various laws instituting direct taxes (on wealth and industry). His proposed income tax is not yet accepted.
1894	Expedition of General Vetter against Lombok (East Indies), where he captures the famous "Treasures of Lombok".
1894	Founding of the Social Democratic Workers Party (SDAP) by Troelstra, Schaper, etc., who oppose the anti-parliamentary anarchism of the other Socialists, such as Nieuwenhuis. Formation of the Association for Female Suffrage.
1896	Passage of Voting Bill of S. van Houten, which increases the franchise to about 50% of the total adult male population. Founding of the Roman Catholic People's Party in Utrecht (R.K.S.P.).

1897   Nationalization of the private telephone companies (In
                1928 the postal, telephone and telegraph systems are
                merged into one state agency, the PTT).

1897-   The cabinet of Pierson and Goeman Borgesius passes a
1901   series of social reform bills:
                    1) the 11-hour work day instituted.
                    2) 10-hour work day instituted for railway workers.
                    3) Also laws passed governing child labor, labor
                       conditions in mines, public health and dwellings.

1898   September. Coronation of Queen Wilhelmina.

1898-   General Van Heutsz finally manages to pacify Atjeh and
1904   thus all of what is present-day Indonesia came defini-
                tively under Dutch rule.

1900   Bill providing for compulsory education passed by very
                narrow margin (50-49).

                The Dutch gunboat "Gelderland" fetches President Kruger
                (of the Orange Free State) from South Africa (During the
                Boer War, the Netherlands is violently anti-British but
                dares not intervene).

1901   February 7. Queen Wilhelmina marries 25-year-old
                Hendrik, Duke of Mecklenburg-Schwerin.

1901-   Kuyper forms a cabinet consisting of a Protestant-Catho-
1905   lic coalition.

1902   The Dutch government offers its services as mediator to
                England and South Africa.

1903   A successful strike in Amsterdam, supported by rail-
                road workers, leads Kuyper to pass laws prohibiting
                strikes by employees of government-owned industries.

1905   Kuyper's Higher Education Bill, providing
                    a) the polytechnical school in Delft becomes an institu-
                       tion of higher learning,
                    b) sectarian universities and high schools receive the
                       right to administer state-approved examinations.

1906   Establishment of the Dutch Association of Trade Unions
                (NVV), a reformist organization linked to the Socialist
                Party (SDAP).

1907   Creation of the Royal Shell group, through a merger of
            Royal Dutch Petroleum and the English Shell Company.

            Second Peace Conference in the Hague, during which the
            cornerstone was laid for the Peace Palace (completed
            1913).

1908   Conflict with Venezuela over Curacao.

            Establishment of the Christian Historical Union by con-
            servative dissidents from Kuyper's Anti-Revolutionary
            Party.

1908   Founding of Budi-Utomo, the first Indonesian nationalist
            movement.

1909   April. Birth of Princess Juliana, future queen.

            Founding of the Christian National Trade Union and of the
            Roman Catholic Labor Bureau.

1912   Foundation of the Sarekat Islam, a Mohammedan national-
            ist organization in Indonesia.

1914   August 1. General mobilization of the army, due to the
            beginning of World War I. General C. J. Snijders made
            commander-in-chief.

            November. England and Germany declare the North Sea
            dangerous waters, making it extremely difficult for
            neutral Dutch shipping. Numerous Dutch ships were tor-
            pedoed by German submarine or blown up by British mines.

1915   Introduction of income tax.

1916   March-April. Rumors of a planned British invasion of
            Belgium leads to a panic concerning the then certain in-
            vasion of the Netherlands by the Germans.

1917   February 1. Germany announces its unrestricted sub-
            marine war, bringing even greater damage to Dutch
            shipping.

            November. Constitutional reform:
            1) Introduction of universal manhood suffrage.

2) Conditions for eligibility for the upper and lower house made the same.
3) Introduction of compulsory voting.
4) Introduction of proportional representation in its most extreme form.
5) Establishment of equal subsidies for state and religious elementary schools.

1918 March. The Allies commandeer the entire Dutch merchant fleet. The Dutch have to submit, as they are dependent on the allies for the import of grain.

November 10. Kaiser Wilhelm flees to the Netherlands, where he is given asylum. The Dutch refuse to turn him over to the Allies.

November 11. At a meeting in Rotterdam, Troelstra urges the working class to seize power. In spite of working class demonstrations in which people are killed (Amsterdam), the revolution does not materialize.

BETWEEN THE WORLD WARS (1918-1939)

1918 Opening of the Popular Council in the Indies, an assembly consisting of Dutch, Arabian, Chinese and Indonesians. The council was limited to an advisory role in government.

Because of the revolutionary mood in the Indies, Governor General van Limburg promises reform and sets up a commission for this object.

1919 February. Belgium demands Dutch territory and a canal from the Rhine for Antwerp.

Women are granted the right to vote.

Minister Aalberse passes the Invalid Law, insuring workers against possible injuries and disabilities. Labor laws are also passed introducing the 8-hour day and 45-hour week and prohibiting the employment of children under 14.

Establishment of the Royal Air Lines Corp. (KLM).

1920	Founding of the Communist Party in the Dutch East Indies.

The Netherlands joins the League of Nations.

The request of the Allies to have Kaiser Wilhelm extradited is definitely refused.

The De Visser Bill formalizes the total equality of public and parochial elementary schools.

1922   Constitution Reform, providing
    a) Succession to the throne limited to the legitimate descendants of Queen Wilhelmina.
    b) The term "colonies" was abolished and the overseas colonies were henceforward to be known as the Dutch East Indies, Surinam and the Dutch Antilles.
    c) Universal female suffrage now made part of the constitution.
    d) Possibilities were created for the passage of laws protecting conscientious objectors from the draft.
    e) War may only be declared with the approval of the States General.

1923   Labor Differences Bill, establishing a state board of labor arbitrators to negotiate between workers, employers in cases of strikes or insoluble differences.

1924   Van der Hoop makes the first airplane flight to the Dutch East Indies.

1925   The Catholic Workers Union (RKWV) is formed.

1926-   Communist and nationalist revolt on Java and Sumatra.
1927   The leaders arrested and interned in New Guinea.

1927   Sukarno forms the Indonesian National Party (PNI), with a purely nationalist program.

The upper house refuses to ratify the agreement with Belgium which gives Antwerp a canal to the Rhine.

1929   Unilever formed through merger of Van den Bergh's
Netherlands Margerine Union and the British firm, Lever
Brothers.

The Netherlands signs the Kellog-Briand Pact, rejecting
war as a means of international diplomacy.

The government arrests the leaders of Sukarno's PNI
and interns them.

1931   Founding of the Dutch National Socialist (Nazi) Party, by
A. A. Mussert and C. van Geelkerken. In 1932 it began
to publish the weekly Folk and Fatherland and established its youth division, the "Youth Storm". By 1933 it
began to attract a number of members.

English pound devalued, but guilder maintained at its old
level. Imports are drastically restricted to combat the
economic crisis.

1932   State Dairy Fund set up to assure minimum prices for
dairy farmers for the duration of the Depression.

Completion of the dike closing off the Zuyder Zee from
the North Sea, the initial step in the drainage of the
Zuyder Zee.

1933   Mutiny on board the cruiser, "The Seven Provinces".
Firm new laws prohibiting civil servants' membership
in subversive organizations (several left-wing organizations affected, but not the Dutch Nazis, the NSB). The
wearing of political uniforms or decorations is forbidden,
a ruling which does affect the Nazis.

1934   July. Riot in the Jordaan section of Amsterdam because
of the lowering of welfare payments to the unemployed.

1935   Big election gains for the Dutch Nazis (NSB), who receive
8% of the total vote, due to the Depression and unemployment.

Founding of "Unity through Democracy", an anti-com-
munist, anti-fascist movement by Geyl and Schermerhorn;
soon the organization has 30,000 members.

Unemployment at its height. In the winter 40% of the labor force is unemployed.

1936   After years of defending the guilder, the Dutch government is forced to follow the devaluation of the pound, dollar and franc.

The Popular Council in the Netherlands Indies accepts the Sutardjo petition calling for a roundtable discussion of a proposition giving the Indies autonomy at the end of ten years. The Minister of Colonies, Welter, refuses to consider the motion.

Law forbidding paramilitary organizations.

1937   Electoral defeat for the Dutch Nazis, resulting in only 4 seats for the party in the lower house. The party remains in decline until 1940.

Publication begins of De Waag (the Scale), financed by Sir H. Deterding, retired chairman of the board of Shell, advocating friendship with Nazi Germany, and espousal of right-wing authoritarian ideas.

Marriage of Crown Princess Juliana with Prince Bernhard of Lippe-Biesfeld.

1938   January 31. Birth of Crown Princess Beatrix.

1939   The cabinet of Premier de Geer takes office, the first Dutch cabinet to contain socialists.

August 5. Birth of Princess Irene.

1939   August 28. Queen Wilhelmina and King Leopold of Belgium offer the great powers their services as negotiators in the hopes of still averting war. General mobilization ordered.

September 3. France and England declare war on Germany as a result of the invasion of Poland.

THE SECOND WORLD WAR (1940-1945)

1940   May 10. German units invade the Netherlands at various
                points, and German paratroopers capture important
                bridges and airfields.

                May 11. Germans take the province of North Brabant.

                May 13. The Queen and the government leave for Eng-
                land.

                May 14. Rotterdam surrenders after a German ultimatum
                but is nevertheless heavily bombed.

                May 15. Capitulation of the Dutch army, with the ex-
                ception of those troops in Zeeland.

                May 29. Seyss-Inquart appointed Reichs Commissioner
                for the Netherlands; gives a conciliatory speech in the
                Hague.

                July. Foundation of the Netherlands Union, to supply an
                alternative to the Dutch Nazi Party.

                Many resistance groups formed, some underground
                papers are published. Gradually the underground begins
                its important work of hiding political refugees and Jews,
                and spying and sabotage.

1941   Founding of the Irene Brigade of Free Dutch troops in
                England. The Dutch navy and merchant marine had al-
                ready been mobilized in the war effort.

                February 25. General strike in protest against the be-
                ginning of the persecution of the Jews. Strike is brutally
                supressed.

                October - December. Establishment by the German
                occupation of compulsory Nazi-oriented organizations
                for all Dutch farmers, artists and physicians.

                December 8. The Netherlands declares war on Japan
                after the Japanese attack on Pearl Harbor.

1942   January. Japanese landing on Borneo (Dutch East Indies).

               February 15. Japanese landings on Sumatra after fall
               of Singapore.

               February 27. Admiral Doorman loses the Battle of the
               Java Sea because of the lack of air support; he is conse-
               quently unable to stop the Japanese landings on Sumatra.

               March 9. Dutch forces on Java capitulate to the Japanese.
               Governor General Tjarda van Starkenborch-Stachouwer
               imprisoned. All Dutch are put in concentration camps.

               July. The Germans begin to deport Dutch Jews, suppos-
               edly to work in Germany and Poland, but actually to be
               taken to the death camps at Auschwitz, Ravensbruck and
               Neuengamme. This process resulted in the death of some
               100,000 Dutch Jews.

               December 7. Queen Wilhelmina promises in a radio
               speech to hold a conference with the Indonesians after
               the war to work out Indonesia's independence within the
               framework of the Empire.

1943   April. The Germans require all Dutch students to take
               a loyalty oath to the Nazis. The 85% who refuse are
               forced to go underground or be deported to work in
               Germany.

               April 29. The Germans take as prisoners of war all
               members of the Dutch army and Navy, whom they had
               previously let free as "brother Germanic folk". The
               general strike that results is brutally supressed by exe-
               cutions.

               Fall. The many armed resistance groups organize them-
               selves into a central movement, the LKP.

1944   September 5. The Netherlands signs the "Benelux"
               accord with Belgium and Luxemburg, aiming at the
               establishment of free trade in the area.

               September 5. "Crazy Tuesday". Unfounded rumors cir-
               culate that the Allies are about to free the Netherlands.
               The Dutch Nazis and Germans flee to the east.

September 17. Allied paratroopers attempt to secure the bridges at Nijmijgen, Eindhoven and Arnhem. At Arnhem the Allies suffer one of the worst defeats of the war. A successful rail strike is begun to aid the Allies, but the consequent requisitioning by the Germans of all waterborne transport causes a critical shortage of food in the west, the "Hunger Winter" of 1944-45.

October 1. The town of Putten is wiped out as a reprisal for an attack on a German armored car. All its male citizens are transported to German concentration camps, from which few return.

October. Liberation of North Brabant, North Limburg and Zeeland.

1945   March 23. Beginning of the great offensive in the north-west. By April 18th, the east and north of the Netherlands were free of German troops.

April 29. The Allies and the German commander in the Netherlands agree to Allied food droppings for the civilian population.

May 5. The German General Blaskowitz, signs the German surrender at Wageningen in the presence of Prince Bernhard and the Canadian General Foulkes.

AFTER WORLD WAR TWO (1945-1959)

June. Formation of the cabinet of Schermerhorn and Drees which instates an emergency Parliament consisting of the members of the pre-war Parliament and certain leaders of the resistance movement.

August 17. Sukarno and Hatta proclaim the independence of Indonesia two days after the capitulation of Japan. Since there were no Dutch forces on the islands, the Japanese surrendered their weapons to the nationalists.

October 31. Negotiations begin with the leaders of the Indonesian Republic.

The emergency Parliament at the Hague ratifies the charter of the United Nations; the Netherlands has thus been a member nation since the U.N.'s inception.

1946   January - February. Dutch Captain Westerling commits
                     war crimes in his brutal pacification of the South Celebes
                     (East Indies).

                     February 9. Founding of the Dutch Labor Party (PvdA)
                     by a coalition of former Socialists, Free Democrats and
                     Christian Democrats.

                     June. First election after the War. The Communists
                     gain, and the Labor Party wins 29 of the 100 seats. The
                     Labor Party Leader, Drees, becomes prime minister of
                     a coalition cabinet in which the Catholic party is the
                     strongest partner.

                     April. Conference between representatives of the Neth-
                     erlands and Indonesia yields no results.

                     July. Malino Conference. The Dutch are in control of
                     Borneo and the eastern archipelago and they are trying
                     to make them parts of a Netherlands-Indonesian Union.

                     November 15. Linggadjati Accord, whereby the Nether-
                     lands recognizes the Indonesian Republic as de facto
                     sovereign of Java and Sumatra. A federal democratic
                     state is to be founded, and the Netherlands-Indonesian
                     Union is set up.

1947   Announcement of the Marshall Plan for the reconstruction
                     of post-war Europe. For the Netherlands this aid was
                     of critical importance.

                     Drees Provisional Bill, giving a pension to all the elderly,
                     including those who have not paid pension premiums.

                     In the Hague, a more detailed protocol is signed by the
                     Benelux nations, providing for the substitution of each
                     land's various duties on imports from abroad by a
                     common schedule of duties on these imports.

                     The Netherlands becomes a member of the U. N.
                     Security Council for the first time.

                     June 8. The Republic of Indonesia accuses the Nether-
                     lands of bad faith in the carrying out of the Linggadjati
                     Accord, since the Dutch refuse to let the Indonesians in-
                     corporate New Guinea into their Republic and are

forming small states in the territory they occupy. The Dutch demand an end to all hostilities and governmental reform.

June 20 - August 5. First Dutch Police Action in Indonesia. Dutch occupy large parts of Java and Sumatra, but they are forced by the U.N. Security Council to stop their actions, and the U.N. begins to negotiate between the belligerents.

1948 January 17. The Linggadjati Accord is confirmed by the Dutch and Indonesians on board the U. S. Renville.

June 24. Formation of the Liberal Party - classical liberals, i.e., conservatives - known as the VVD, by former members of the Freedom Party and the Labor Party.

September 4. Queen Wilhelmina abdicates in favor of her daughter, Juliana. With the title of princess, she retires to her palace at the Loo.

September 6. Coronation of Juliana.

The Benelux nations become members of the Organization of European Economic Cooperation, a necessary step for full participation in the benefits of the Marshall Plan. The Benelux lands also join the West European Union, a military pact between England, France and the Benelux.

December 10 - January 5, 1949. Second Police Action on Sumatra and Java. The U.N. Security Council forces the Dutch to free the prisoners it has taken and to cease hostilities.

First Round Table Conference between the Netherlands, the Netherlands Antilles and Surinam leads to the decision to form a United Kingdom of the Netherlands with the Netherlands and Surinam full members.

1949 The Netherlands take part in the founding of the North Atlantic Treaty Organization (NATO) for a common defense against the Communist threat from Eastern Europe.

August - November. Indonesia and the Netherlands take part in a Round Table Conference at the Hague to draw up the transfer of sovereignty. New Guinea is simply left out of the transactions.

December 27. Transfer of sovereignty over Indonesia from the Netherlands to the Republic of Indonesia signed at Amsterdam and Batavia (henceforth Djakarta).

1950   January 23. An attack on Bandung by the Dutch Captain, Westerling, gives the Republic of Indonesia an opportunity to begin its campaign to annex the independent federated states set up by the Dutch on the smaller Indonesian islands. The Republic of the South Moluccas on the island of Ambon resists the Republic's attempts and ask the Dutch for aid. Aid is refused, but all the Ambonese who prefer to live in the Netherlands are given free passage to Rotterdam.

December. Fruitless conference between the Indonesian Republic and the Netherlands over the New Guinea question.

1951   January. Government crisis caused by the rejection of prime minister   Stikker's Indonesian policy by his own Liberal Party. Drees returns as prime minister.

The Netherlands and Belgium join the European Coal and Steel Community, which was designed to create a common market for these commodities.

1952   Unemployment bill gives compulsory unemployment insurance to all employees.

Second Round Table Conference between the Netherlands, the Netherlands Antilles and Surinam. Problems emerge over the possibility of secession.

June. Elections, in which the Labor Party gains seats, a result of the popularity of "Father Drees".

1953   February 1. The islands in Zeeland and South Holland are inundated as the result of a terrible storm. Over 1,300 people are lost and great damage is done to property. It takes a year to close the dikes; ultimately

a drastic new dike-building plan (called the Delta Plan)
will be developed in 1957 for the protection of the
islands.

1954   The Catholic bishops of the Netherlands address a
            pastoral letter to Dutch Catholics criticizing secular
            tendencies and the relations of Catholics with Socialist
            organizations.

            Third Round Table Conference between the Netherlands,
            the Netherlands Antilles and Surinam. Promulgation of
            the Statute of the Kingdom.

1956   October 13. Drees forms his fourth cabinet, ending what
            was, until the 1972-1973 crisis, the longest government cri-
            sis in Dutch history, which had begun on June 13, 1956.

            Unilateral withdrawal of Indonesia from the Round Table
            Conferences with the Netherlands.

1957   January. Founding of the Pacifist Socialist Party, which
            was critical of the involvement with NATO of the regular
            Socialists.

            Announcement of the Delta Plan, of which the final goal
            is the closing off of all the Zeeland inlets, except for
            the Western Scheldt.

            Introduction of general pension plan for the elderly
            (A.O.W.), replacing the provisional bill.

            The six members of the European Coal and Steel Com-
            munity, including the Netherlands and Belgium, sign the
            Treaty of Rome, setting up the European Economic
            Community - better known as the Common Market - and
            Euratom, a European atomic energy community.

1958   The Drees government resigns, ending the period of
            post-war government by coalition of labor and religious
            parties which designed the post-war recovery and indus-
            trialization and made the extensive program of social
            legislation possible.

1959   March. General election, leading to the ...

May. De Quay cabinet, the first post-war cabinet not containing a member from the Labor Party. The De Quay cabinet is a reaction against previous strong government intervention in economic affairs.

Bill to aid widows and orphans of employees.

THE UNRULY SIXTIES AND SEVENTIES

1960   April. The Netherlands signs a settlement with West Germany. The Netherlands gives back some German territory, and Germany pays 280 million marks as compensation to Dutch war victims.

Diplomatic relations broken off between the Netherlands and the Republic of Indonesia. Indonesia begins its policy of military confrontations with the Netherlands on the island of New Guinea.

1961   July. Introduction of the 5-day work week for government employees.

New Round Table Conference with Surinam and the Netherlands Antilles over reforms in their status and government.

The Netherlands strongly supports England's efforts to join the Common Market against de Gaulle's veto.

1961-   Dutch statesman, D. U. Stikker, Secretary-General of
1965   NATO.

1962   November 29. Death of former Queen Wilhelmina.

1963   Elections, again resulting in the formation of a centrist cabinet without Labor Party members.

General Welfare Law passed, replacing previous poverty bills; the new law rests on the concept that state aid to the poor is not a favor but a constitutional right.

A new treaty with Belgium aiming at giving Antwerp a better connection with the Rhine through the Netherlands.

May 1. Transfer of sovereignty over New Guinea from the Netherlands to Indonesia. The population of New Guinea would be given a chance to decide about its government before 1969. Diplomatic relations are restored between Indonesia and the Netherlands.

1964   Princess Irene marries Prince Carlos-Hugo of Bourbon-Parma, the leader of the Spanish Carlists, in Rome without having asked the consent of the States General; after turmoil in Parliament, Irene forfeits her rights to the throne.

1965   February. Formation of a new government, including the Labor Party. As an indication of growing Dutch concern with the Third World, a new Ministry, that of Foreign Aid in Development, is included in the new cabinet.

May 25. Foundation of Provo, first a magazine, then a group of young Amsterdam anarchists who aim at challenging all existing authority in a whimsical manner.

1966   March 10. Marriage of Crown Princess Beatrix with the German Claus von Amsberg leads to serious riots.

June 14-15. Riots of the Amsterdam construction workers, resulting in the death of one man, leads to the dismissal of Mayor van Hall of Amsterdam.

October. Publication of Ten Over Red by the "New Left" group, demanding
   a) the ending of the monarchy after the death of Juliana,
   b) Dutch resignation from NATO if Portugal were to remain a member,
   c) leveling of the differences in income,
   d) tuition-free state education.

October 9. Publication of the New Catechism, revealing the progressive turn of Dutch Catholicism in the 60's.

October 14. The Catholic Party brings down the Catholic-Socialist government, but suffers a split in its ranks in doing so.

1967   General elections result in heavy losses for the Catholic and Labor Parties. A newly-formed party, D'66 which wants a 2-party system that offers a clear choice, gets a surprisingly strong vote. The new cabinet is based on the three confessional parties and the liberal party.

1968   March. Formation of the Radical Political Party (PPR) by dissident left-wing former members of the Catholic and Protestant Parties.

1969   January. Meeting of the Dutch Pastoral Council, where Catholic lay and clergy try jointly to hammer out a new leadership for the Church.

Student revolts at the Business School at Tilburg and the University of Amsterdam in order to force through democratization of higher education.

May. Strikes at the oil refineries on Curacao leads to rioting, and, on the request of the Antilles government, the Dutch marines are sent in to restore order.

1970   At a new meeting of the Pastoral Council, the bishops are asked by the laity to separate celibacy from the institution of priesthood.

State visit of President Suharto of Indonesia.

1971   State visit of Queen Juliana to the Republic of Indonesia confirms the new policy of Dutch-Indonesian friendship and cultural exchange.

MEMBERS OF THE HOUSE OF ORANGE
WHO SERVED AS STADTHOLDERS
OF HOLLAND AND ZEELAND DURING THE TIME OF THE REPUBLIC

William of Orange	1559–1567 and 1572–1584
Maurits	1585–1625
Frederick-Henry	1625–1647
William II	1647–1650
(First Stadtholderless Period)	1650–1672
William III	1672–1702
(Second Stadtholderless Period)	1702–1747
William IV	1747–1751
William V	1751–1795

SOVEREIGNS OF THE HOUSE OF ORANGE-NASSAU

King William I	1813–1840
King William II	1840–1849
King William III	1849–1890
Queen Emma, regent	1890–1898
Queen Wilhelmina	(1898–1948)
Queen Juliana	1948 –

FAMILY TREE OF THE SOVEREIGNS
OF THE HOUSE OF ORANGE-NASSAU

William I — (1772-1843), King of the Netherlands 1815-1840; married 1) Wilhelmina of Prussia and 2) Henriette d'Oultremont.

William II — (1792-1849), King of the Netherlands 1840-1849; married Anna Pavlovna of Russia.

William III — (1847-1890), King of the Netherlands 1849-1890; married 1) Sophia of Wurttemberg, 2) Emma of Waldeck-Pyrmont.

1) William (1840-1879)

1) Maurits Alexander (1843-1850)

1) Alexander (1851-1884)

2) Wilhelmina (1880-1962). Queen of the Netherlands 1890-1948; married Duke Henry of Mecklenburg. Juliana (born 1909), Queen of the Netherlands since 1948; married Bernhard of Lippe-Biesterfeld.

Beatrix (born 1938) married Claus von Amsberg

William-Alexander (born 1967)

Irene (born 1939) married Carlos Hugo of Bourbon-Parma

Margriet (born 1943) married Pieter van Vollenhoven

Christina (born 1947)

CABINETS IN THE NETHERLANDS
SINCE THE INTRODUCTION OF
PARLIAMENTARY RESPONSIBILITY IN 1848

Donker Curtius–de Kempenaer   1848–1849

1st Thorbecke   1849–1853

2nd van Hall   1853–1856

van der Brugghen   1856–1858

Rochussen–van Bosse   1858–1860

3rd van Hall   1860–1861

Van Zuylen–van Heemstra   1861–1862

2nd Thorbecke   1862–1866

Fransen van der Putte   1866

Heemskerk–van Zuylen   1866–1868

Van Bosse–Fock   1868–1871

3rd Thorbecke   1871–1872

De Vries–Fransen van der Putte   1872–1874

2nd Heemskerk   1874–1877

Kappeyne van de Coppello   1877–1879

Van Lijnden van Sandenburg   1879–1883

3rd Heemskerk   1883–1888

Mackay (coalition)   1888–1891

Can Tienhoven–Tak van Poortvliet
(liberal)   1891–1894

Roell-van Houten (liberal)	1897-1901
Pierson-Goeman Borgesius (liberal)	1897-1901
Kuyper (coalition) De Meester-Van Raalte (liberal, extra-parliamentary)	1905-1908
Heemskerk (coalition)	1908-1913
Cort van der Linden (lib., extra-parliamentary)	1913-1918
1st Ruys de Beerenbrouck (coalition)	1918-1922
2nd Ruys de Beerenbrouck (coalition)	1922-1925
1st Colijn (coalition)	1925-1926
1st De Geer (coalition, extra-parliamentary.)	1926-1929
3rd Ruys de Beerenbrouck (extraparliamentary., coalition.)	1929-1933
2nd Colijn (extraparlimentary, coalition & liberal)	1933-1935
3rd Colijn (extra parliamentary, coalition & liberal)	1935-1937
4th Colijn (extraparliamentary, coalition & liberal)	1937-1939
5th Colijn (Protestants, liberal and extraparliamentary)	1939
2nd De Geer (broad base & Socialists)	1939-1940
Gerbrandy (many changes)	1940-1945
Schermerhorn-Drees (emergency cabinet)	1945-1946

1st Beel-Drees (Socialists, R. C.)	1946-1948
1st Drees (broad basis)	1948-1951
2nd Drees (broad basis)	1951-1952
3rd Drees (broad basis)	1952-1956
4th Drees (broad basis)	1956-1958
2nd Beel (interim cab.)	1958-1959
DeQuay (coalition & VVD)	1959-1963
Marijnen (coalition & VVD)	1963-1965
Cals (PVDA, KVP, ARP)	1965-1966
Zijlstra (interim cabinet)	1966-1967
De Jong (coalition & VVD)	1967-1969
1st Biesheuvel	1969-1972
2nd Biesheuvel	1972-

DOCUMENT I

The Dutch national anthem was written during the Revolt of the Netherlands. It has the form of a narrative of the tribulations of Prince William of Orange, as recounted by himself. It was used by the rebels as a marching song. The following are five of the fifteen stanzas:

William of Nassau scion
    Of a Dutch and ancient line,
I dedicate undying
    Faith to this land of mine.
A prince I am, undaunted,
    Of Orange, ever free.
To the King of Spain I've granted
    A lifelong loyalty.

A shield and my reliance
    O God, Thou ever wert.
I'll trust unto Thy guidance,
    O leave me not ungirt,
That I may stay a pious
    Servant of Thine for aye,
And drive the plagues that try us
    And tyranny away.

O David, thou soughtst shelter
    From King Saul's tyranny.
Even so I fled this welter
    And many a lord with me.
But God the Lord did save him
    From exile and its hell.
And, in His mercy, gave him
    A realm in Israel.

Nothing so moves my pity
    As seeing through these lands
Field, village, town and city
    Pillaged by roving bands.
O that the Spaniards rape thee,
    My Netherland so sweet,
The thought of that does grip me
    Causing my heart to bleed.

Alas, my flock, to sever
    Is hard on us.   Farewell.
Your Shepherd wakes, wherever
    Dispersed you may dwell.
Pray God that He may ease you,
    His gospel be your cure.
Walk in the steps of Jesu.
    This life will not endure.

DOCUMENT II

In 1566 the Revolt of the Netherlands began with riots all over the country aimed mainly at the churches and monasteries, where the religious images and altars were destroyed. The following is a report of the riots of Antwerp, written by an envoy of the English court:

It was the marveylest pece of work that ever was sene done in so short a tyme; and so terybell in the doing, that yt wolde make a man afrayd to thinke uppon it,---being more lyke a dreme than such a piece of work.

And whereas it was well allowed, in a manner, of all men, the pulling down of the Images,---it is dislyked of most men that they have made such a spoil as they have done, in stelyng all the golde, sylver, and jewells within the church; and breking up of dores where they had nothing to doo. They have spoiled not only the evydens of all the churches, but the evydens of many in this town; who had brought their evydens into the church for fere of fyre, or other. As also, whereas there was many faire sepoultures made in the churches, they have broken and defased them all: so that by this menes and other, the prechers ar come much into the derision of the pepell. God turn all to the best! for that presently we are here in grett perplexity att thys present,---all men one afrayde of another; and nott without cause, for that the nomber of the poore are so much--abell to be master over the other. So that and if there were not very good watch and warde, it were not other [than] possybell but that all should go to ruine here. And for the avoydyng thereof, the whole towne hath watched night and day ever since thys business began; and must do, for a tyme; for that now there are many taken that have taken of the silver and jewels out of the church, who shall be putt to execution; where about, I doubt will be muche adoo. . . .

The Protestants are not to be blamed; for that, so far as I can lerne, there was not one that was put to worke of purpose, that has taken the worth of a penny: but the hurt that was done, was done by vacabonds that followed. Whereof some of our nation are blamed, and not without cause; for here are a great nombre in this towne that are fled out of England for robbyng and such lyke, and [these] kept such a stir in this spoil! --- more than enough.

In this towne, all kind of merchandise is at a stey; and most men of reputacion [are] fled abrode into all places: for that, of all lykelyhood, thys matter cannot be well endyd, but that thys towne shall be in danger to be spoiled; for that all the vakabonds of the country draweth to this towne. God send us quyetness!

Syns the begynning of thys my letter, they write from Brussells that the Regent hath made answer to the gwessys [gueux,] weche ys to their contentment; and [that] ys, that the whole matter ys comitted to the order of the Prince of Orange, the county of Egmont, and the county of Horne, tyll such tyme as that the great states of this country do meet; whiche hath not beene in [four-score yeres, nor cannot well be done in a yere or so. So that thys ys that they have desired for; and yf any men by the procurement of the court, should take upon them to reforme any of these matters, either by forse or otherwyse, these nobellmen maye by authority take part against them. So that there ys good hope that all shall be well. And now, since thys great falle of Babylon, the prechers that were wont to preche without, prech now within the towne; and begonne, as yesterday, in the forenoon, (beyng appointed by the Lords,) one to preche in St. George's church, one in the Boro' church, and one in the Black-Friars. But when they came to the Friars, they shut the dors, and wolde not suffer them to enter: whereupon the pepell wolde have brokyn down the dors, but the precher wold not, at no hand, that they should do [so] ; and so went into the new town by the Esterlinge Howse, and prechyd: but the other two prechyd in the churches."

So that now there ys good hope that all shall be well. And whereas in the great spoile dyvers pieces of alters stood, as allso the xii apostells about the church, which had cost a great sum of money, (every picture att the least x foote high,) the Lords have causyd them to be pullyd down and broken in pieces, and all other images that remained. As also they have caused all the alters to be brokyn in pieces, and the alter-stones, some of towche and some of marbell, brokyn in pieces. So that, so far as I can perceive, they will leeve nothing in the church whereof any memory should be; and all the stuff of that wych ys broken, the Lords have given to the masters of the poor, which ys worth a greet piece of monny allthough it be brokyn. For I dare say that the garnyshing of our Lady Church had cost above 200,000 marks; for there was dyvers alters that had cost 5,6, and 700L . . . . . .Before my next, I think all the Netherlands will be made clere."

Syns the ending of this my letter (being Sunday, at viii of the clocke,) the prechers of the word of God go to their sermons in the new word of God go to their sermons in the new towne: whereupon the prysts, thinking not to have over [?] this openyd all the churches and began to preche. Whereupon dyvers stood up and said this their doctryne was false doctryne: whereupon was lyke to have come a fowle piece of work. Whereupon the Lords sent unto them their offysers, commanding them not only to leve preching, but also to shut up their churches, or else they wold. So that the prysts wyll not leve thys, till they have sought so well their owne destruction, as of their images; for as I do understand, and yf they be not quyett, and that they do seke any further business, some of the Captains have said that they wyll not leve one pryst or frere alyve in the country.

DOCUMENT III

In the fall of 1576 the States General, representing most of the Netherlands, joined the revolution which William of Orange had kept going in the provinces of Holland and Zeeland. The following excerpt is from Orange's speech to the assembly of the States General, November, 1576.

"You will be an example of virtue to all free peoples, and you will inflict terror upon all tyrants and unjust oppressors of republics; you will leave to posterity a most worthy and most useful example for the protection of the privileges and freedom, in the same way as did our ancestor . . . thus you will give to posterity the just and legitimate basis of its firm and unchangeable freedom, which is in obedience only to a just and legitimate prince; doing this you will give its due to your conscience, to the obligation of your oath and the position you hold, representing the universal body of the whole people, whose freedom and welfare you hold in trust."

DOCUMENT IV

In 1581 the rebels finally deposed Philip II of Spain as their sovereign. The Bill of Abjuration, an eloquent justification of this action, became a model for the later English and American revolutionary declarations.

The States General of the United Provinces of the Low Countries, to all whom it may concern, do by these Presents send greeting:

As 'tis apparent to all that a prince is constituted by God to be ruler of a people, to defend them from oppression and violence as the shepherd his sheep; and whereas God did not create the people slaves to their prince, to obey his commands, whether right or wrong, but rather the prince for the sake of the subjects (without which he could be no prince), to govern them according to equity, to love and support them as a father his children or a shepherd his flock, and even at the hazard of life to defend and preserve them. And when he does not behave thus, but, on the contrary, oppresses them, seeking opportunities to infringe their ancient customs and privileges, exacting from them slavish compliance, then he is no longer a prince, but a tyrant, and the subjects are to consider him in no other view.

And particularly when this is done deliberately, unauthorized by the States, they may not only disallow his authority, but legally proceed to the choice of another prince for their defence. This is the only method left for subjects whose humble petitions and remonstrances could never soften their prince or dissuade him from his tyrannical proceedings; and this is what the law of nature dictates for the defence of liberty, which we ought to transmit to posterity, even at the hazard of our lives. And this we have seen done frequently in several countries upon the like occasion, whereof there are notorious instances, and more justifiable in our land, which has been always governed according to their ancient privileges, which are expressed in the oath taken by the prince at his admission to the government; for most of the Provinces receive their prince upon certain conditions, which he swears to maintain, which, if the prince violates, he is no longer sovereign. Now thus it was with the king of Spain after the demise of the emperor, his father, Charles the Fifth, of glorious memory (of whom he received all these Provinces), forgetting the services done by the subjects of these countries, both to his father and himself, by whose valor he got so glorious and memorable victories over his enemies that his name and power became famous and dreaded over all the world, forgetting also the advice of his said imperial majesty, made to him before the contrary, did rather hearken to the counsel of those Spaniards about him, who had conceived a secret hatred to this land and to its liberty, because they could not enjoy posts of honor and high employments here under the States as in Naples, Sicily, Milan, and the Indies, and other countries under the king's dominion. Thus allured by the riches of the said Provinces, wherewith many of them were well acquainted, the said counsellors, I say, or the principal of them, frequently remonstrated to the king that it was more for his majesty's reputation and grandeur to subdue the Low Countries a second time, and to make himself absolute (by which they mean to tyrannize at pleasure), than to govern according to the restrictions he had accepted, and at his admission sworn to observe. From that time forward the king of Spain, following these evil counsellors, sought by all means possible to reduce this country (stripping them of their ancient privileges) to slavery, under the government of Spaniards having first, under the mask of religion, endeavored to settle new bishops in the largest and principal cities, endowing and incorporating them with the richest abbeys, assigning to each bishop nine canons to assist him as counsellors, three whereof should superintend the inquisition. By this incorporation the said bishops (who might be strangers as well as natives) would have had the first place and vote in the assembly of the States, and always the prince's creatures at devotion; and by the addition of the said canons he would have introduced the Spanish inquisition, which has been always as dreadful and detested in these Provinces as the worst of slavery, as is well known, in so much that his imperial majesty, having once before proposed it to these States, and upon whose remonstrances did desist, and entirely give it up, hereby giving proof of the great affection he had for his subjects.

Having also, after the decease of Don John, sufficiently declared by the Baron de Selles that he would not allow the pacification of Ghent, the which Don John had in his majesty's name sworn to maintain, but daily proposing new terms of agreement less advantageous. Notwithstanding these discouragements we used all possible means, by petitions in writing, and the good offices of the greatest princes in Christendom, to be reconciled to our king, having lastly maintained for a long time our deputies at the Congress of Cologne, hoping that the intercession of his imperial majesty and of the electors would procure an honorable and lasting peace, and some degree of liberty, particularly relating to religion (which chiefly concerns God and our own consciences), at last we found by experience that nothing would be obtained of the king by prayers and treaties, which latter he made use of to divide and weaken the Provinces, that he might the easier execute his plan rigorously, by subduing them one by one, which afterwards plainly appeared by certain proclamations and proscriptions published by the king's orders, by virtue of which we and all officers and inhabitants of the United Provinces with all our friends are declared rebels, and as such, to have forfeited our lives and estates. Thus, by rendering us odious to all, he might interrupt our commerce, likewise reducing us to despair, offering a great sum to any that would assassinate the Prince of Orange. So, having no hope of reconciliation, and finding no other remedy, we have, agreeable to the law of nature in our own defence, and for maintaining the rights, privileges, and liberties of our countrymen, wives, and children, and latest posterity from being enslaved by the Spaniards, been constrained to renounce allegiance to the King of Spain, and pursue such methods as appear to us most likely to secure our ancient liberties and privileges. Know all men by these presents that, being reduced to the last extremity, as above mentioned, we have unanimously and deliberately declared, and do by these presents declare, that the King of Spain has forfeited, ipso jure, all hereditary right to the sovereignty of those countries, and are determined from henceforward not to acknowledge his sovereignty or jurisdiction, nor any act of his relating to the domains of the Low Countries, nor make use of his name as prince, nor suffer others to do it. In consequence whereof we also declare all officers, judges, lords, gentlemen, vassals and all other the inhabitants of this country of what condition or quality soever, to be henceforth discharged from all oaths and obligations whatsoever made to the King of Spain as sovereign of those countries. . . .And to cause our said ordinance to be observed inviolably, punishing the offenders impartially and without delay; for so 'tis found expedient for the public good. And, for better maintaining all and every article hereof, we give to all and every of you, by express command, full power and authority. In witness whereof we have hereunto set our hands and seals, dated in our assembly at the Hague, the six and twentieth day of July, 1581, indorsed by the orders of the States-General, and signed J. De Asseliers.

DOCUMENT V

Around the turn of the century the Dutch tried everywhere to attack the Spanish-Portuguese monopoly of Asian trade. Their great guide was Jan van Linschoten, who had gone to Asia in Portuguese service and published a description of the Spanish-Portuguese colonial empire after his return. The following sections are from his Itinerario (1598).

a: from Chapter I.

Beeing young, and living idlelye in my native Countrie, sometimes applying my selfe to the reading of Histories, and straunge adventures, wherein I tooke no small delight, I found my minde so much addicted to see and travaile into strange Countries, thereby to seeke some adventure, that in the end to satisfie my selfe, I determined, and was fully resolved, for a time to leave my Native Countrie, and my friendes (although it greeved me) yet the hope I had to accomplish my desire, together with the resolution, taken in the end overcame my affection and put me in good comfort, to take the matter upon me, trusting in God that he would further my intent. Which done, being resolved, thereupon I tooke leave of my Parents, who as then dwelt at Enckhuysen, and beeing ready to imbarke my selfe, I went to a Fleet of ships that as then lay before the Tassell, staying the winde to sayle for Spaine, and Portingale, where I imbarked my selfe in a ship that was bound for S. Lucas de Barameda, beeing determined to travaile unto Sivill, where as then I had two bretheren that had continued there certaine yeares before: so to help my selfe the better, and by their meanes to know the manner and custome of those Countries, as also to learne the Spanish tongue.

b: Linschoten's description of Java

Through this straight or narrowe passage Thomas Candish an Inglish captaine passed with his Ship, as he came out of the south parts, from Nova Spaigne. This Iland aboundeth with Rice, and all manner of victuals, [as oxen,] kyne, hogges, sheepe, and hennes, [etc also] Onyons, Garlicke, Indian nuttes, [and] with al [kind of] Spices, as cloves, Nutmegges, and mace, which they carry unto Malacca. The principall haven in the Iland is Sunda Calapa, whereof the straight beareth the name: in this place of Sunda there is much Pepper, and it is better then that of India or Malabar, whereof there is so great quantitie, that they could lade yearlie from thence 4 or 5 thousand kintales Portingale waight: it hath likewise much frankinsence, Benioin of Bonien called Folie, Camphora, as also Diamantes, to which place men might very well traffique, without any impeachment, for that the Portingales come not thether, because great numbers of Iaua come themselves unto Malacca to sell their wares.

And although it be besyde the matter, yet doe I not esteeme it unnecessary in briefe to shewe, in what sort they use to buy, sell, and deall with ware, money and waight, seing we are now in hand with the [said] money then certaine copper mynt called Caixa, of the bignes of a Hollandes doite, but not half so thicke, in the middle whereof is a hole to hang it on a string, for that commonlie they put two hundreth or a thowsand upon one [string] , wherewith they knowe how to make their accounts, which is as followeth. 200 Caixas is a Sata, and 5 Satas are 1000 Caixas, which is as much as a Crusado Portingale money, or 3 Keysars guilders, Netherlandish money, Pepper of Sunda is solde by the sacke, and each sacke wayeth 45 Catten waight of China: everie Catte is as 20 Portingale ounces, and everie sacke is worth, as it is solde there, 5000 Caixas, and when it is at the highest, 6 or 7 thowsand Caixas, Mace, Cloves, nutmegges, white and black Beniamin, and Camphora, are solde by the Bhar, each Bhar of Sunda weigheth 330 Catten of China. Mace that is good is commonlie worthe 100 or 120 thowsand Caixas, and good Cloves after the rate, but [bad or] foule Cloves of Baston are worth 70 or 80 thowsand Caixas the Bhar. Nutmegges are commonlie worth 20 or 25 thowsand Caixas the Bhar: white and black Benioin is worthe 150 and 180 thowsand Caixas, and 200 thousand the Bhar. The wares that are there [by them] desired in barter for their spices, are as hereafter followeth, divers and different sorts and colours of cotton lynnen, which come out of Cambaia, Choramandel and Bengala, as Sarasses de Gabares, and painted Tapen from S. Thomas, of fyve elles [the peece] : they are clothes so called out of Bengala, white Cotton lynnen, viz. Sarampuras, Cassas, Sateposas, and blacke Satopasen, and some browne unbleached lynnen: out of Cambaia black Cannequiins, red Turiaes, which are all clothes of cotton lynnen, red Beyramen great and litle, which is verie like unto Cambricke: and I am perswaded, if Clothe [of Holland were there to be soulde,] it woulde be more esteemed than Cotton lynnen out of India. These Javens are of a verie fretfull and obstinate Nature, of colour much like the Malayers, brown, and not much unlike the men of Brasilla, strong and well set, big limmed, flatte faces, broad thicke cheekes, great eyebrowes, smal eyes, little beard, [not past] 3 or 4 hayres upon the upper lippe and the Chinne: the hayre on their heades very thyn and short, yet as blacke as pitche, whose picture is to be seen by the picture of the Malayen of Malacca, because they dwell and trafficke much together.

DOCUMENT VI

Apart from the route around the Cape of Good Hope, the
Dutch tried to find an alternative passage to the Indies via the
Arctic Sea. During one of those attempts Willem Barents and
his crew were stranded for a long polar winter on the island of
Nova Zembla. The Diary of one of the shipmates, Gerrit de
Veer, from which the following sections have been taken, became
one of the most popular travelbooks of the Dutch.

a: The crew celebrates New Year and Twelvenight in the house they
have improvised.

The 31 of December it was still foule wether with a storme out of the
north-west, whereby we were so fast shut up into the house as if we had
beene prisoners, and it was so extreame cold that the fire almost cast no
heate; for as we put our feete to the fire, we burnt our hose before we could
feele the heate, so that we had [constantly] work inough to do to patch
our hose. And, which is more, if we had not sooner smelt then felt them,
we should haue burnt them [quite away] ere we had knowne it.

[Anno 1597]

After that, with great cold, danger, and disease, we had brought the
yeare unto an end, we entered into y yeare of our Lord God 1597, y beginning whereof was in y same maner as y end of anno 1596 had been; for the
wether continued as cold, foule, [boisterous] , and snowy as it was before, so that upon the first of January we were inclosed in the house, y wind
then being west. At the same time we agreed to share our wine euery
man a small measure full, and that but once in two daies. And as we were
in great care and feare that it would still be long before we should get
out from thence, and we sometimes hauing but smal hope therein, some
of us spared to drink wine as long as wee could, that if we should stay long
there we might drinke it at our neede.

The 2 of January it blew hard, with a west wind and a great storme,
with both snow and frost, so that in four or five daies we durst not put our
heads out of y doores; and as then by reason of the great cold we had
almost burnt all our wood [that was in the house] , notwithstanding
we durst not goe out to fetch more wood, because it froze so hard and
there was no being without the doore; but seeking about we found some
[superfluous] pieces of wood that lay ouer the doore, which we [broke
off and] cloue, and withall cloue the blocks whereon we used to beate our
stock-fish, and so holp our selues so well as we could.

The 3 of January it was all one weather [constantly boisterous, with
snow and a north-west wind, and so exceedingly cold that we were forced
to remain close shut up in the house] , and we had little wood to burne.

The 4 of January it was still foule stormie weather, with much snow
and great cold, the wind south-west, and we were forced to keepe [con-

stantly shut up] in the house. And to know where the wind blew, we
thrust a halfe pike out at y chimney w a little cloth or fether upon it; but
[we had to look at it immediately the wind caught it, for] as soone as
we thrust it out it was presently frozen as hard as a peece of wood, and
could not go about nor stirre with the wind [so that we said to one another
how tremendously cold it must be out of doors] .

The 5 of January it was somewhat still and calme weather. Then we
digd our doore open againe, that we might goe out and carry out all the
filth that had bin made during the time of our being shut in the house, and
made euery thing handsome, and fetched in wood, which we cleft; and it was
all our dayes worke to further our selues as much as we could, fearing lest
we should be shut up againe. And as there were three doores in our
portall, and for y our house lay couered ouer in snow, we took y middle
doore thereof away, and digged a great hole in the snow that laie without the
house, like to a side of a vault, wherein we might go to ease our selues and
cast other filth into it. And when we had taken paines al day, we remem-
bered our selues that it was Twelf Even, and then we prayed our maister
that [in the midst of all our troubles] we might be merry that night, and
said that we were content to spend some of the wine that night which we
had spared and which was our share euery second day, and whereof for
certaine daies we had not drunke; and so that night we made merry and
drunke to the three kings. And therewith we had two pound of meale
[which we had taken to make paste for the cartridges] , whereof we
[now] made pancakes with oyle, and [we laid to] euery man a white
bisket which we sopt in [the] wine. And so supposing that we were in
our owne country and amongst our frends, it comforted us as well as if
we had made a great banket in our owne house. And we also made tickets,
and our gunner was king of Noua Zembla, which is at least two hundred
800 miles long and lyeth betweene two seas.

b. The 24th of January they see the sun which they had not seen
since November 4th:

The 20 and 26 of January it was misty and close weather, so y we
could not see anything. Then they that lay d y contrary wager w us, thought
that they had woon; but upon the twenty seuen day it was cleare [and
bright] weather, and then we [all] saw the sunne in his full roundnesse
aboue the horison, whereby it manifestly appeared that we had seene it upon
the twenty foure day of January. And as we were of diuers opinions touching the same, and that we said it was cleane contrary to the opinions of all
olde and newe writers, yea and contrary to the nature and roundnesse both
of heauen and earth; some of us said, that seeing in long time there had
been no day, that it might be that we had ouerslept ourselues, whereof we
were better assured: but concerning the thing in itselfe, seeing God is
winderfull in all his workes, we wille referre that to his almightie power,
and leaue it unto others to dispute of. But for that no man shall thinke us to
be in doubt thereof, if we should let this passe without discoursing upon it,
therefore we will make some declaration thereof, whereby we may assure
our selues that we kept good reckening.

You must understand, that when we first saw the sunne, it was in the
fift degree and 25 minutes of Aquarius, and it should haue staied, according

to our first gessing, till it had entred into the sixteenth degree and 27 minutes of Aquarius before he should haue shewed there unto us in the high of 76 degrees.

Which we striuing and contending about it amongst our selues, we could not be satisfied, but wondred thereat, and amongst us were of oppinion that we had mistaken our selues, which neuerthelesse we could [not] be persuaded unto, for that euery day without faile we noted what had past, and also had used our clocke continually, and when that was frosen we used our houre-glasse of 12 houres long. Whereupon we argued with our selues in diuers wise, to know how we should finde out that difference, and learne the truth of the time; which to trie we agreed to looke into the Ephemerides made by Josephus Schala, printed in Venice.

c. Late in spring they prepare boats to try to find a way out. The skipper dies.

The 18 of June we repaired and amended our scutes againe, being much bruised and crushed with the racking of the ice, and were forced to driue all the nailes fast againe, and to peece many things about them, God sending us wood wherewith we moult our pitch, and did all other things that belonged thereunto. That done, some of us went upon the land to seeke for egges, which the sick men longed for, but we could find none, but we found foure birds, not without great danger of our liues betweene the ice and the firme land, wherein we often fell, and were in no small danger.

The 19 of June it was indifferent weather, the wind north-west, and [during the day west and] west south-west, but we were still shut up in the ice and saw no opening, which made us thinke that there would be our last aboade, and that we should neuer get from thence; but on the other side we comforted our selves againe, that seeing God had helped us oftentimes unexpectedly in many perils, and that his arme as yet was not shortened, but that he could [still] helpe us at his good will and pleasure, it made us somewhat comfortable, and caused us to speake cheerfully one unto the other.

The 20 of June it was indifferent weather, the wind west, and when the sunne was south-east [1/2 p. 7 a.m.] Claes Adrianson began to be extreme sicke, whereby we perceiued that he would not liue long, and the boateson came into our scute and told us in what case he was, and that he could not long continue aliue; whereupon William Barents spake and said, I thinke I shal not liue long after him; and yet we did not iudge William Barents to be so sicke, for we sat talking one with the other, and spake of many things, and William Barents read in my card which I had made touching our voiage, [and we had some discussion about it] ; at last he laid away the card and spake unto me, saying, Gerrit, give me some drinke; and he had no sooner drunke but he was taken with so sodain a qualme, that he turned his eies in his head and died presently, and we had no time to call the maister out of the [other] scute to speake unto him; and so he died before Claes Adrianson [who died shortly after him] . The death of William Barents put us in no small discomfort, as being the chiefe guide and onely pilot on whom we reposed our selues next under God; but we could not striue against God, and therefore we must of force be content.

The 21 of June the ice began to driue away againe, and God made us some opening with [a] south south-west wind; and when the sunne was [about] north west the wind began to blow south-east with a good gale, and we began to make preparations to go from thence.

The 22 of June, in the morning, it blew a good gale out of the south-east, and then the sea was reasonable open, but we were forced to draw our scutes ouer the ice to get into it, which was great paine and labour unto us, for first we were forced to draw our scutes ouer a peece of ice of 50 paces long, and there put them into the water, and then againe to draw them up upon other ice, and after draw them at the least 300 paces more ouer the ice, before we could bring them to a good place, where we might easily get out. And being gotten into the open water, we committed our selues to God and set saile, the sunne being about east-north-east, with an indifferent gale of wind out of the south and south-south-east, and sailed west and west and by south, till the sunne was south, and than we were round about enclosed with ice againe, and could not get out, but were forced to lie still. But not long after the ice opened againe like to a sluce and we passed through it and set saile againe, and so sailed along by the land, but were presently enclosed with ice; but, being in hope of opening againe, meane time we eate somewhat, for the ice went not away as it did before. After that we used all the meanes we could to breake it, but all in vaine; and yet a good while after the ice opened againe [of itself] , and we got out and sailed alonga by the land, west and by south, with a south wind.

DOCUMENT VII.

The seventeenth century saw the development of a typical Dutch form of Republicanism. Pieter de la Court's The Interest of Holland (1662) was the classical statement of anti-monarchism, religious toleration and economic liberalism. The following sections are from the English translation of 1702.

a: From Chapter IX about the flourishing of commerce and the people.

I suppose it to be evident, that the eighth part of the Inhabitants of Holland could not be supplied with Necessaries out of its own product, if their Gain otherwise did not afford them all other necessaries: So that Homo Homini Deus in Statu Politico, one Man being a God to another under a good Government, it is an unspeakable Blessing for this Land, that there are so many People in it, who according to the Nature of the Country are honestly maintain'd by such sutable or proportionable means, and especially that the welfare of all the Inhabitants (the idle Gentry, and Foreign Soldiers in pay excepted) from the least to the greatest, does so necessarily depend on one another . . . . However, this excellent and laudable Harmony and Union may be violated, even to the Ruin of all the Inhabitants, none excepted but Courtiers and Soldiers, and that by one sole mistake in Government, which is the Electing one Supreme Head over all these Inhabitants, or over their Armys. For seeing such a single Person for the increase of his Grandeur, may curb and obstruct Holland's Greatness and Power, by the Deputies of the lesser Provinces of the Generality, who also may in their Course check the great and flourishing Cities in their own Provincial Assemblies, by the Suffrages or Votes of the envious Gentry. And the lesser Cities, and the great Persons, Courtiers and Souldiers being all of his Party, and depending on him, must needs prey upon the industrious or working Inhabitants, and so will make use of all their Power for their own benefit, and to the detriment of the Commonalty. And to the end they may receive no let from the great and strong Cities of Holland, it follows that they would either weaken or lessen all such Cities, and impoverish the Inhabitants, to make them obedient without control. Which if so, we have just cause continually to pray, A furore Monarcharum libera nos Domine; God preserve Holland from the Fury of a Monarch, Prince, or one Supreme Head. But what there is of reality in this, shall be handled hereafter in a Chapter apart.

b: From Ch. XVIII about freedom of Religion.

Having hitherto spoken of four considerable ways of preserving the Prosperity of Holland, I think it not fit to go over any more tending to the fame end, till I first briefly hint how Holland hath governed itself as to the said Expedients. And first as to freedom of Religion, it is certain that having till this time been greater in Holland than any where else, it hath brought in many Inhabitants, and driven out but few; yet it is also certain, that since the Year 1618, we have begun to depart from that laudable Maxim more and more.

First with the Remonstrants, persecuting them by Placaets, Fines, and Banishments, and driving them into other Lands: Afterwards with the Romanists. . . . This is no less unreasonable, than detrimental to the Land: For if we cannot spare the Benefit which accrues to us by their Abode and Traffick, why should we prohibit that which is not hurtful to the State, and whereof the Romish Inhabitants make so great Account, and without which they cannot dwell amongst us? If we permit none but small Assemblies in Cities, in the Houses of known Citizens, with such Priests as are best approved of by the Rulers, that Inconvenience would have an end, and Peace and Friendship increase more and more among the good Inhabitants, yea and the true Religion too. And moreover, our State would avoid that Vexation which now by disturbing those prohibited Meetings may happen: And on the contrary, the State could incur no danger by those well known Assemblies, where every one might have free Access, and no matter of secrecy could be consulted of; but the Publick Safety would every way be better secured. But what shall we say? not only the Politicians, but also the Clergy are Men; and commonly the sweet Temper of such as have suffer'd under Persecution is changed into Force and Violence, so soon as they become Masters of others: then they forget the Evangelical Lesson, and the Law of Nature, to do nothing to others but what they would have done to themselves; and on the contrary, they remember and practice that old tyrannical and accursed Maxim, As he hath done to me, so will I do to him; and he that hath the Power, let him use it.

c: From Part II, Ch. XII.
        That Holland during its Free Government, cannot be ruined by any
        Intestine Power.

It is evident that no Domestick Power can subvert the Republic of Holland, nor destroy the Welfare of the Inhabitants, except by a general Conspiracy, Sedition, Insurrection, and Civil War of the People and Citys of Holland against one another, because they are so wonderfully linked together by a common Good, that those homebred Tumults and Wars are not to be supposed able to be raised, except by Inhabitants of such eminent Strength, as is able to force the Magistracy of the Country to the execution of such destructive Counsels. And seeing now in Holland and West-Friesland there is no Captain-General or Stadtholder, nor any Illustrious Person except the Prince of Orange; therefore we will consider, whether if the said Prince who is in no Office of the Generality, continuing in these Provinces, might be able to cause or effect such ruinous and destructive Divisions in Holland . . . . .

Perhaps some may say, that the Rulers or States of this Province, of their own accord, or seduced by Promises and Gifts, forget that warning, Fear those who are accustomed to do ill, especially when they make Presents*; and will bring in the Trojan Horse. But yet the arm'd Men conceal'd in his Belly, will never be able, by the Conspiracy of some Magistrates, to destroy our Province, and to subdue and burn our Citys by Uproars against the Rulers; but possibly they may by bringing in the Horse, weaken our lawful Governors, and leave our Citys without defence, and then the Horse may be drawn into the inward Court, and into the feeble and weak Assembly of the States. As Ruy Gomaz de Silva says of the Netherlands in general; "That they are more fiery than they should be for the preservation of their Libertys, when by force they are attempted to be taken from them; and yet never any People have been so easy almost wholly to resign them. And the Emperor Charles to the Fifth used to say, That no People were so averse from Servitude as the Netherlanders, and yet in the World no People suffered the Yoke to be so easily laid on them, when they were gently treated. Besides which Cardinal Bentivoglio endeavours to shew by many Reasons, That the United Netherland Provinces cannot long preserve their free Government; but seeing the Netherlanders have never before been in the quiet possession of a Free Republick, at least not the Hollanders, there can be no Example given of their neglecting their own Freedom, or of corrupting them with Mony for that end. For when formerly it happened in Holland by unavoidable sad Accidents, that we were necessitated to draw the Trojan Horse into inward Court, we saw the Fire and Flame snorting, neighing, and armed Men spring from his Body at pleasure, without regard either to the Benefit or Damage of the Inhabitants. So we shall always find it true, in all chargeable and necessitous Countrys, governed by a few Aristocratical Rulers, and provided with but few unrewarded annual Magistrates, That a great Person obtaining there any Power in the Government or Militia, will easily draw to his Party all Rulers and Magistrates by the most considerable and profitable Offices and Benefices which he can confer; or if any dare to stand it out against him, he would keep him out of employment, or deter him from maintaining the Publick Liberty: So that every one to obtain those Advantages, or to evade those Hardships, will be tempted to give up the Freedom of his Country; and it is no wonder that we have seen such dealings so often practiced in these Parts.

But it is also true, that when the Princes of these Countrys were raised to such a degree, that they conceiv'd it was no longer needful for them to oblige the Rulers and Magistrates of the Gentry, and Citys, not doubting to bear them down by their great Popularity among the Inhabitants, or to suppress them by their Military Authority; it hath often appeared, that beyond expectation many good Patriots, and lovers of Liberty, especially many prudent, ancient, and experienced Merchants, have then evidenced their Zeal for the defence of their Privileges, well knowing they should be forced to part with them under a Monarchical Government; and therefore joined with such Rulers and Magistrates as encourag'd them to maintain their Freedom, as far as they possibly could, nay even the shadow of Liberty, with their Lives and Fortunes.

All which ought to perswade us, that the Assembly of the States of Holland, and the subordinate Magistrates of this present Free State, having in their own Power the bestowing of all honourable and profitable Employments; and which is more, not needing now to fear their own Military Power, and being able without scruple to command them, and by them to reduce other mutinous and seditious Inhabitants to obedience, will not now be inclined to call in, or set up a Head, which they would immediately fear no less than Idolaters do the Idols of their own making; and not only so, but they must reverence his Courtiers too, and beseech them that they would please to suffer themselves to be chosen and continued in the yearly Magistracys, and bestow some Offices and Employments on them and their Friends, changing the Liberty they now enjoy as Magistrates of a Free State, into a safe and slavish dependence. Which things well considered, we ought to believe that the Hollanders will rather chuse to hazard their Lives and Estates for the preservation of this present free Government.

DOCUMENT VIII

When the Dutch Republic in the eighteenth century became a more and more oppressive oligarchy under the Prince of Orange the new democratic ideas attacked both the Prince and the oligarchy. The following is from the Manifesto of the democratic movement, the pamphlet To The Dutch People, written by Joan van der Capellen tot den Pol in 1781.

. . . . Netherlanders, arm yourselves and attend to the affairs of the whole country, because they are your own affairs. The country belongs to all of you together and not only to the Prince and his cronies who consider you, all of us, the whole people of the Netherlands, the descendants of the free Batavians, like hereditary property, and treat us like oxen and sheep which they can shear and butcher as they like. The people which inhabit a country, the burghers and farmers, poor and rich, big and small, all of them together, are the real proprietors, the masters of the country: they have the right to decide how they want to be governed . . . the people in government, the Prince or whoever exerts any power in the country does that only in your name. All their power comes from you. You are the shareholders, the owners, the masters, of this national corporation which has established itself under the name of the United Netherlands in this region. The people in government are only the executives of that company. You pay them out of your own purse, they are your servants, subject to your authority, accountable and obedient to you alone. Again, all people are born free. By nature nobody has power over another individual . . .

Are we lacking in respect to you, William IV of Orange, if we suspect that you strive for higher authority, if we suspect that the old civil authority no longer satisfies you, that you will not rest before you bear a crown? . . . . Is not the conduct of your personal life beastly, adding to the sorrow of your sensible and honorable Princess? Does one not see you drunk in public every day, a target of ridicule and contempt for everybody?. . . .

People of the Netherlands, cherish the freedom of the press, since it is the only support of your national liberty. If one cannot speak freely with the other citizens, if one cannot warn them in time, the work of the oppressor becomes very easy . . . Arm yourselves, elect the men who must be in command and proceed calmly and modestly (like the people of America, where not a drop of blood flowed before they were attacked by the English); Jehova, the God of freedom, who led the Israelites out of servitude and made them a free people, will support our just cause.

People of the Netherlands, dear compatriots,
I am your faithful citizen,

Ostende
September 3, 1781.

DOCUMENT IX

When Napoleon's Empire began to desintegrate in 1813, the English
government began to think about a larger role for the Netherlands
in a reconstructed Europe. The following document is Lord
Castlereagh's memorandum about this issue to the allies.

"MEMORANDUM RESPECTING HOLLAND,
submitted to the Powers end of 1813"

As the splendid successes in Saxony render it probable that the French
may shortly be compelled to retire behind the Rhine, the British government
are desirous of inviting the attention of their allies to the importance of
directing their early efforts to the expulsion of the enemy from Holland.

From the best information they have been able the procure, the people
of Holland are ripe for revolt as soon as the allied armies shall be in a
situation to protect their first movements.

The general feeling of the nation, it is stated, inclines them to recur
to their antient Institutions, with some changes especially calculated to give
more vigour to the Executive Power, -- and as the British Government are
also assured, they with one voice call for the restoration of the Orange
Family.

In order to be prepared to assist such an effort from hence, authority
has been given to the Prince of Orange to levy in the North of Germany a
small corps (2000 Infantry) of Dutch, amongst the prisioners and deserters.
They are to be enrolled under H. S. H.'s auspices, and to bear the name of
the Family. It is proposed to attach this corps to the force in British pay,
now serving with the Prince Royal's army, till the moment shall arrive for
detaching and giving more extension to it.

In addition to this commencement of an army, 20.000 stand of arms
are embarked, and held in constant readiness in the Downs, to be landed at
the shortest notice in Holland wherever required.

This arrangement has been confidentially notified to those persons in
the interior of Holland who are in communication with this country.

As the allied Powers will be probably desirous, in looking to the
restoration of Holland, to be informed of the views entertained by the British
Government on this important subject, there can be no hesitation in stating
them in a general manner, and with as much precision as can be adopted
with respect to an arrangement, which must in a great measure take its
colour from the other stipulations to be made upon a general Peace.

The Rhine being specified, in the secret Articles to the Defensive
Treaties lately concluded by the Allies, as the boundary to be required from
France, it has afforded the British Government great satisfaction to have

received official assurance, that they do not consider themselves as thereby precluded from proposing and insisting upon those arrangements which may be necessary to the general system of Europe in modification of that outline.

In point of fact the Rhine never was insisted upon even by France as a boundary to Holland, whilst that State was suffered to retain even the semblance of independence. If the object is now to re-establish Holland in a situation both as to territory and frontier to sustain its independence, the British Government submit to the consideration of the Allies, that if this is the object, the territories of the United Provinces as they stood in the year 1792 cannot possibly admit of the smallest reduction.

If things can be restored on the side of the Low Countries to a state, similar to that in which they stood at that period, when one of the great military Powers of Germany was interposed as a protection between France and Holland, the British Government will not feel it necessary to press for any departure from the antient arrangement of limits; but if the course of events should be such as to render this highly desired object unattainable; and the frontier of France should still remain in contact with that of Holland, they feel it essential that Antwerp, with such other extension of territory as may be necessary to give to the United Provinces an adequate military frontier, should be assigned to Holland.

They do not feel that it can be necessary to enter more minutely at the present into the details of such an arrangement; they confine themselves to the statement of the general principle, short of which they do not conceive that Holland can be placed in any reasonable state of security.

After the various communications which have taken place with the Allies on this point, it is unnecessary to urge at any length the extreme importance it is to the interests of the continent that Holland should be severed from France. If in no other point of view than as the natural centre of the money transactions of Europe, all independent nations are interested in its being again raised to the rank of a free and independent State. But if the necessity of narrowing the hostile frontiers of France towards Germany is considered, it becomes still of more vital consequence, especially to the Northern States, that this country full of resources, strongly covered with defenses, and opening numerous débouchés by which a French army may at once penetrate into the heart of Germany, should be wrestled from France.

It also deserves the most serious consideration (a view of this great question in which all the Continental Powers are equally interested) that unless material reduction can be effected in the extent of coast which France occupies at present, and in her means of naval equipment, England will be obliged to turn all her attention and resources to the increase of her marine, and will be comparatively unequal to assist the continent in any future struggle to which it may be exposed, either with troops or money.

In doing justice to the principles, which, throughout this long and arduous contest, have invariably actuated this country, the Powers of the continent will no doubt feel interested in upholding the strength and influence of a Nation which has so perseveringly devoted all its faculties to re-establish on a firm and lasting basis the independence of other nations.

The immediate object of this Memorandum is to point the active and early efforts of the Allies to the recovery of Holland. Whenever matters may be ripe for entering more fully upon its future settlement, the British Government will be prepared to recur to those principles which were laid down in a despatch to Lord Cathcart of. . . . . with respect to the Colonies conquered from Holland since 1803, which despatch has been actually communicated to the Allies, with a sincere disposition on their part, liberally to strengthen Holland in proportion as that important portion of Europe can be rendered secure by adequate arrangements against the Power of France.

DOCUMENT X

IX. On the 18th of November, 1813, in the last days of the French occupation, a revolutionary committee in the Hague took over with the following proclamation establishing monarchy in the Netherlands; the patronizing tone is characteristic:

Long live the House of Orange! Holland is free. The Allies are marching on Utrecht. The English are coming. The French are fleeing and everywhere the sea is open. Trade is restored. All party strife has ended. All suffering is forgotten and forgiven. All the notables will be given office. The government proclaims the Prince sovereign. We are joining the Allies and forcing the enemy to make peace. There will be a holiday at public expense but there will be no looting nor violence. Everyone thanks God. The old times are coming back. Long Live the House of Orange!

DOCUMENT XI

During the February Revolution of 1848 in France, King William II turned, as he himself expressed it, a liberal in twenty-four hours. The result was a liberal constitution largely inspired by the liberal leader Thorbecke. The constitution was somewhat too liberal for the needs of the rather backward and conservative Netherlands. One gets an interesting idea of the composition of Parliament in the following letter from the English envoy Lord Napier to his government.

The Hague 12th December 1860.

My Lord,

The provinces which now form the kingdom of the Netherlands have maintained from the remotest times some form of government, embodying an element of municipal and popular freedom. Those liberties have, no doubt, been unequally shared between town and country, and the different classes of the people in both, they have been overshadowed by the prerogative of counts, emperors and stadtholders, they have even suffered a transitory suppression by a foreign, though not unprofitable usurpation, but they have proved their stubborn vitality by ever springing up anew, and they are now enjoyed and administered with greater harmony and efficacy than at any previous period.

The French tyranny was a sharp remedy, but a necessary one, and eventually beneficent, for it levelled the superannuated structure of local laws, customs, and constitutions, introduced a regular code, perfected religious toleration, and blended the whole nation in common suffering, and a common passion for renovation and independence.

Under the first sovereign of the House of Orange, the old principles of political representation were embodied in forms adapted to the requirements of the age, but the development of a working parliamentary government was arrested partly by the popular and indefatigable character of the king, who was invested with almost absolute authority by the affection of his northern subjects, and partly by the antagonism of the Dutch and Belgians, which split the legislative body into two fractions, divided, not so much by a reasonable diversity of opinions on political subjects as by religious and national animosities.

The rupture of the kingdom in 1830, the financial embarrassments and efforts which ensued, the declining influence of the sovereign, and his eventual retirement combined to promote the ascendancy of the Chamber, the country became ripe for a constitutional change, and the crisis of 1848 afforded an opportunity for revising the organic statute of 1815, and founding representative institutions on a broader basis.

It may be affirmed that the virtual government of the Netherlands had passed to the Second Chamber of the States General. The royal family still preserves a traditional respect, and could, by obeying generous impulses, or using politic arts, awaken a warm popular sympathy, but the assembly has obtained an habitual grasp of power of which it could not easily be deprived. This power is used with prudence for the people, and with deference to the throne, it gives no scandal to the partisans of freedom, and no offence, to the reasonable votaries of monarchical authority.

The members of the Second Chamber of the States General, 72 in number, are chosen by 38 electoral districts.

The basis of representation is ostensibly laid, not in local interests and natural bounds, but in population. One member is allotted to 45.000 inhabitants. The numerical principle, justly applicable in conjunction with universal suffrage, is hardly consistent with a property qualification, under which the members, who represent the same number of souls, may not represent the same number of voters. The law mitigates this defect by modifying the electoral qualification according to the circumstances of the district, making it higher in the richer, and lower in the poorer regions of the kingdom. The remedy is not altogether effectual, but the proportion is approximatively preserved throughout, of one member to about 1.200 voters.

The right to vote is contingent on the payment of direct taxes, and thus with some exceptions, on the possession of real property. Mere tenancy at will, or under ordinary leases, to whatever value, mere funded wealth to whatever amount, the defence of the state, or the exercise of a learned profession, give no claim to the franchise. In the most opulent cities, the electoral qualification implies a payment of at least fl. 112, about £9.10.0, in direct taxes. In the most indigent boroughs, the test is reduced as low as fl. 20 or £1.14.0. In the fertile country districts of Holland, Zealand and Utrecht, the highest rate is fl. 40, equal to £3.10.0, and it sinks ,in the wilds of Drenthe, and the islands of Friesland to half that sum.

The electoral qualification is consequently high in amount and limited in character, though settled in the year 1848, at a moment of ardent excitement and under a liberal administration. It was probably designed to secure a constituency both respectable and independent, identified with positive obligations to the state, and inaccessible to the influences of government, capital and the great land owners.

Under this stringent, and exclusive law there were in the Netherlands in 1858 89.376 persons entitled to the parliamentary franchise, affording one voter to about 37 inhabitants. In ordinary times, about half this number go to the poll, in periods of extreme agitation nearly the whole electoral body has been called into action. The Dutch are little disposed to take a busy and sustained part in politics. They rather enjoy their liberties, than exercise their rights. Some vital questions must be at stake, affecting the conscience, the heart, or the purse of the nation, to rouse them to exertion. The Pope, or the House of Orange, the finances or the colonies, must be in question; then the masses are stirred to an active participation in public affairs.

The members of the Second Chamber are elected for four years. Half the Chamber is discharged at the end of every two years, an expedient by which it is kept in course of regular and certain renewal. The right of extraordinary dissolution is reserved to the crown, but is rarely exerted.

The members receive a salary of about £180 per annum, and an allowance for travelling expenses.

The Netherland assembly cannot be as well divided into distinct parties as the English Parliament, or the American Congress.

In the inclosed table I have made an attempt to class the deputies according to the prevailing tenor of their sentiments, not according to their current votes, for no great question involving the higher principles of politics is now before the country, and voting for, or against the ministry affords no test when the ministry has no real political complexion, and is not of one mind.

According to my estimate formed under the counsels of a leader of the opposition, and those of a confidant of the court, there are at present in the Second Chamber, 18 reactionary conservatives, 20 liberal conservatives, and 34 liberals.

The same return exhibits the religious division of the legislative body, and shows that there are 15 catholic representatives, to 57 protestant. This result is unfavourable to the catholics, who, if represented in proportion to their numbers, would send at least 24 members. Even this imperfect representation of the old religion is due to its' concentration and preponderance in particular provinces; if it was equally diffused, as that of a minority throughout the country, I doubt whether a single catholic deputy would be returned to parliament.

One fraction of the Chamber forms a solid party, cemented not only by conformity of opinions, but also by personal attachments, and obedience to a chief, those liberals, I mean, who recognise the leadership of Mr. Thorbecke, the member for Deventer.

Mr. Thorbecke belongs to the learned class; het filled a chair in the university of Leyden, and has carried the didactic method of schools, into the free arena of the Chamber. His origin, and connections are partly German, his manner is dry, his temper is aspiring, his honesty is unquestionable, his abilities are equally fitted for speculation, and business, he inspires affection among his steady adherents, who may number about sixteen members. Mr. Thorbecke having been called to power in the year 1848, was the chief author of the existing political constitution. He is an object of strong repugnance to the king, to whose will he would never bend, for whose failings he had not sufficient charity, but whose office he always treated with respect.

The liberals not enrolled in the sect of Mr. Thorbecke, and the indifferent herd of conservative liberals, vote independently, every man being ruled by his individual convictions, partialities, and enmities.

Among the protestants there is a small group of evangelical calvinists, the faithful seed of the synod of Dort, whose main vocation is to combat the Pope, and all his works, whose sentiments are commonly reactionary, but who are in truth persons of high attainments, piety and good works. They would strengthen the royal authority and reduce the catholics to a state of subordination. It is interesting to find among these Dutch Orangemen, and orthodox patriots an Aeneas Mackay, still devoted to the race of king William, and professing the opinions which made that sovereign great. The posterity of the mercenary but respectable Highlander have cast their lines in pleasant places, and are blest with temporal gifts in no common measure.

The catholics would no doubt vote together in the cause of religion, but they are not unanimous in political tendencies. Some are really liberal at heart, others vote with Mr. Thorbecke because the strength of the liberal party is propitious to the freedom of their religion, but others are so notoriously fanatical and ultramontane that notwithstanding occasional liberal votes, they must be regarded essentially as reactionaries, and are therefore placed in the same political category with most of their deadly antagonists, the high calvinists. The most influential member among the catholics is Mr. Nispen van Sevenaer, a gentleman of fair character, abilities and estate, but altogether devoted to the interests of his church. Mr. Meylink is a subordinate tool of Rome.

If we turn from the political, and religious constitution of the Chamber, to regard its social composition, we shall find that it comprises the following elements:

Seventeen members connected with the independent profession of the law, as advocates and attorneys.

Ten persons holding judicial offices.

Seven men of aristocratic descent, only two of whom, Amerongen, and Zuylen de Nyevelt, bear names associated with great employments in former times, and distinguished in the history of the United Provinces.

Six gentlemen connected with the army.

Two connected with the navy.

Five directly identified with the interests of commerce and finance.

Two manufacturers.

Twelve landed proprietors, representative men of that class.

Two grazing farmers from Groningen, with the aspect, manners, and sentiments, belonging to that order of democratic rustics, men enriched by the provision trade with England, and made radicals by antagonism to their landlords from whom their farms are leased, in ''emphiteusis'', a kind of everlasting tenure or copyhold.

Two practising physicians.

One retired minister of the gospel, baron van Hoevell, who is the leading philanthropist and colonial reformer in the Chamber.

Finally there are a few members, who cannot be associated with any interest or profession, persons devoted to peculiar studies and pursuits, or without distinctive character, idle and unattached.

Your Lordship will perhaps think the lawyers too numerous, and the merchants and men of family too few. Such is the general impression among reflecting people, who deplore the indifference for politics which prevails with the traders and capitalists of the great cities, as well as among the nobility who live apart, or dedicate themselves to the court.

The Chamber is, with these drawbacks, a fair representation of the wealth, intelligence and morality of the country.

The second branch of the legislature meets in a plain, but convenient hall, in the "Binnenhof", the old town residence of the stadtholders. The president, at present, is Mr. van Reenen, in whom the advantage of an agreeable exterior has not been neglected; he occupies the centre of one of the longer sides. The throne is opposite the speaker's chair. The bench of ministers, who are not representative members, but who attend, and speak, officially, is placed below the throne. The deputies sit at either extremity of the apartment, without any accurate division of parties. The members, who intend to take part in the discussion, inscribe their names previously, on a list preserved by the officers of the House, and are successively called on, to speak from their places. The debates are conducted with much gravity, most of the deputies expressing themselves with a facility which might be envied in England. No applause, or noise of dissent is tolerated. In physionomy and deportment, the members appear rather above than below their origin and avocations.

They would not suffer at all by comparison with the House of Commons, and differ chiefly from our assembly, by the absence of young men, for no one can be elected below the age of thirty, and few are chosen who are not ten years older.

The scene is not very brilliant, nor are the interests debated momentous to the general world, yet the place is memorable in the past, and the present actors are perhaps superior to their diminished part. The decent and useful exercise of popular representation by the Dutch cannot be altogether indifferent to England, nor uninteresting to Her Majesty's government. It is certainly a legitimate object of scrutiny for this legation.

I have the honor . . .

DOCUMENT XII

> In 1940 the German invasion brought the first war in over
> one hundred years to the Netherlands. The following description
> of the first days of the war and the escape to England of the
> Queen and her government is taken from Queen Wilhelmina's
> memoirs, Lonely But Not Alone.*

In May all the reports pointed to an attack within a few days. Ra-
tionally I had to admit this, and yet like so many others I still clung to a
last hope that something entirely unforeseen might happen which would
prevent the worst. But it did not happen!

On the 9th of May, Phaff insisted that we should spend the night in
the air-raid shelter. At four o'clock in the morning the enemy crossed
our frontier. I addressed myself to the nation with the following proclamation:

My People,

After all these months during which our country has scrupulously observed a strict neutrality, and while its only intention was to maintain
this attitude firmly and consistently, a surprise attack without the slightest
warning was launched on our territory by the German armed forces last
night. This in spite of a solemn guarantee that our neutrality would be
respected as long as we maintained it ourselves.

I hereby raise a fierce protest against this unexampled violation of
good faith and outrage upon all that is proper between civilized states.

I and my government will continue to do our duty. You will do
yours, everywhere and in all circumstances, each in the place he occupies, with the utmost vigilance and the inner peace and devotion which a
clear conscience affords.

A few hours after the invasion it was reported to me that the
palace guard had shot down an enemy aircraft, which had crashed in the
neighbouring park. That morning German paratroops dropped over The
Hague in large numbers.

A request reached me from military quarters to leave the Huis ten
Bosch and take up our residence in town, where our personal safety would
be better assured. We arrived at the Noordeinde after an adventurous
journey; confusion everywhere, crowds and traffic jams and bewildered
soldiers, who after their first experience of battle with the enemy paratroopers were hardly able to distinguish between friend and foe . . . . . .

After consultation with those whose opinion should be heard---a
miniature war council in life-jackets---I decided to go to England. This
was allowed by the commander's instructions. From there I thought it
would be possible to renew contact with Holland, and then to decide when
I could return and where I should go. Moreover, it would also be possible
once more to ask for military assistance.

---

*Reprinted by permission of the copyright holder.

Of course I was fully aware of the shattering impression that my departure would make at home, but I considered myself obliged, for the sake of the country, to accept the risk of appearing to have resorted to ignominious flight.

If the guerilla against the parachute troops had not cut off all connections with the army fighting on the Grebbe, I could have joined it to share the fate of the soldier and, as William III put it, to be the last man to fall in the last ditch. I knew that this was not granted to me either.

How different the development of the war was from what we had imagined! A return to the Netherlands became impossible. General Winkelman soon capitulated, as he was empowered to do when further fighting would have meant useless bloodshed.

The destroyer disembarked me and my party at Harwich, where I intended to stay in expectation of my return. The British authorities, however, had already provided a train to take me to London, so I left. At the station I was met by King George and by my children, who were very upset and did not understand that I should have had to follow them so soon. The King asked me to be the guest of himself and the Queen, and escorted me to Buckingham Palace. Bernhard returned immediately to the scene of the fighting in our country and then went on to France. A few days later Haakon and Olav of Norway arrived. Like ourselves, Norway had to give up resistance on her own soil and to continue it at the side of the Allies.

As soon as Hitler's treacherous attack had started, the ministers Van Kleffens (Foreign Affairs) and Welter (Colonies) and had gone to England in order to make contact with our allies. I found them there when I arrived. The other ministers came the day after.

After my arrival in London our proclamation was issued:

When it had become absolutely certain that we and our ministers in the Netherlands could no longer continue to exercise our authority freely, the difficult but inevitable decision had to be taken to transfer the seat of government to a foreign country, for as long a period as will be necessary and with the intention to return to the Netherlands at the first opportunity. The government is now in England. It wishes to avoid a governmental capitulation. Thus all of the Netherlands territory that is still in our hands, in Europe and in the East and West Indies, continues as one sovereign state to make its voice heard in the community of states and particularly in the consultations of the combined allies. The military authority, and in the last resort the Commander-in-Chief, now takes all the measures that are necessary and justified from the military point of view.

The civilian authorities in occupied territory should continue doing everything that can serve the interest of the population and in the first place should help to maintain peace and order.

Our heart goes out to our fellow-countrymen at home, who will live through difficult times. But in the end the Netherlands will recover its entire European territory with God's help. Remember the disasters of former centuries which the country overcame, and do all you can in the best interests of the nation, as we shall on our part. Long live the Fatherland!

DOCUMENT XIII

In February, 1941, Amsterdam led the nation in a strike in protest against the beginning persecution of the Jews by both Dutch and German Nazis. The following is an excerpt from a retrospective report appearing in the (formerly underground) newspaper Het Parool on March 4, 1971:

Tuesday, February 25, early in the morning a strike began which soon became general. The streetcars stopped running, and that appeared to be a signal for most all workers to strike. The large department stores were unable to open, since clerks and delivery personnel were struck. The workers at the Fokker aviation factories struck, and all the industrial workers across the river Y followed their example: this entire Amsterdam industrial center - including the many shipyards and factories working for the Germans - was shut down . . .

The workers of Amsterdam showed what they thought of the anti-Semitic obscenities perpetrated over the previous months by Nazi thugs of German and Dutch origin. A seething indignation filled the city. Were we going to look on passively while our Jewish brothers were beaten up? Were we going to look the other way with the classical question - which cowards always ask in this situation - Am I my brother's keeper? The people of Amsterdam answered: We will defend those who are burdened and oppressed and trampled on . . . Zaandam followed Amsterdam's example; so did factories in Haarlem and in Hilversum.

In all places the strike was primarily a strong protest against the scandalous anti-Semitic terror which the German barbarians started in our country. But it was at the same time a protest against all the other injustices, the lawlessness, the slavery and the slow starvation which the Germans brought upon our country . . . .

The reaction of the Germans showed how they have lost their heads. The German police was sent into the streets in innumerable trucks and they began to shoot everyone who did not get out of the way. Machine guns were brought into position on streetcorners and swept the streets clean. On many occasions hand grenades were used. The gray and green trucks went screeching through the street, machine guns rattled, grenades exploded, and through this din one heard German curses and the hoarse cannibal battle screams of the uniformed Nazis charging into the unarmed masses . . .

The strike's occurrence is of great importance for the remainder of the war. Abroad, friend and enemy understand that the spirit of the Dutch people is unbroken and that we will know how to act at the right moment. The people of the Netherlands know their duty, also in the future. We have every reason to take heart at the events in the capital. But let us not delude ourselves. The Dutch Nazis have been driven off the streets and it has been made clear to the enemy that we shall not bear everything in silence. But the strike is a weapon of limited effectiveness. When, however, we know how to use this weapon in connection with other weapons, it can be powerful and decisive. Let us preserve our forces, waiting for the moment when that becomes possible and let us strike out again when our action will be the most effective. Then, if we keep our powder dry and our swords sharp, we can look to the future with legitimate confidence.

DOCUMENT XIV

In 1944 the South of the Netherlands was liberated, but the North remained under German rule until the end of the war. The following texts come from Queen Wilhelmina's memoirs, Lonely But Not Alone* and describe the situation of 1944-1945, and her first trip into the liberated parts of the Netherlands.

On the 24th of February 1945 I addressed the Dutch people in the customary way with the following words:

Let me begin by reading to you a poem many of you know, because it expresses so well what lives in all of us:

> But if I live to see the liberation
> And cheer the victory parade,
> God, tell me that this suffering,
> This sorrow shall not be betrayed.
>
> And resurrect this nation, finer, wiser,
> Than when it went to meet its fate,
> That we may as free men on earth
> Direct our gaze towards Thy state!
>
> Because by then this land's horizons
> Will bathe in Thy eternal light,
> Because this soil with blood is hallowed
> Shed by Thy martyrs in their fight . . . .
>
> Leave but this land to them forever,
> Let us receive it by their hand!
> Make only what their pains acquired
> Return to be our Fatherland!

Not only is it our bounden duty, but there is burning inside us, a sacred fire compelling us to achieve the fulfilment of the poet's prayer. A fire that will allow no delay in the making of preparations.

Our liberation is coming about in a different way from what we had imagined.

The war has established a temporary frontier along our rivers, thus creating a division of our people, who all during the cruel days of the occupation shared the same fate and were so closely united in joys and sorrows and still are, more than ever before, spiritually one and indivisible.

Whereas all of you north of our rivers are still subjected to the criminal regime of the enemy, who does not even shrink from inflicting starvation upon you, those of you who are already liberated have experienced all the horrors and destruction of war on your own soil, and you have come to

---

*Reprinted by permission of the copyright holder.

know   only too well what it means to be in what the soldier calls an operational area, and you are still waiting for the fulfilment of the wishes and ideas which have sprung up during the years of oppression.

Those who can see deeper than the surface realize at once that the interests of the occupied and liberated Netherlands are identical.

This being so, we as a nation would show bad faith towards the many who sacrificed themselves, going through tortures and suffering in silence, as well as towards our most fervent desire, if we did not set to work, even now, to prepare the new era of our national existence and to pave the way for the times that will follow immediately upon the liberation of our entire people. We must liberate ourselves, as far as possible, not least in the spiritual sense.

In the recently completed reconstruction of the cabinet, this need was taken into account.

I am happy to see that men who are supported by the confidence of the liberated provinces have been found willing to join this cabinet.

In the execution of its difficult task the cabinet will most carefully avoid any measures which require the approval of the nation as a whole. Its duties will come to an end with the liberation of our country. At that moment I hope to arrange for the formation of a cabinet consisting of persons who enjoy the confidence of my whole people.   In anticipation of general elections, as I said on the 10th of May last year, an emergency parliament will be called as soon as possible.

The utmost effort will be made to provide help and a satisfactory food supply for those parts of the Netherlands and the empire that are still awaiting their liberation, and to improve conditions in the liberated areas.

Urged on by my awareness of the need to do all we can to convince our allies of the distress inflicted upon the Netherlands by our ruthless enemies, I have recently followed up many other steps already made by my ministers and myself and informed the King of England and the President of the United States personally of all this, at the same time asking them for the early and effective assistance which is imperatively required to save the situation.   On the foundations of love, justice and truth, we shall work to create the national community whose image lives in us all.

The promising outlook for the war in the Far East should act as a spur to our preparations for taking part in the liberation of the Netherlands East Indies.

It gives me genuine satisfaction to see that so many young people volunteer for this enterprise.   I am filled with justifiable pride by the selflessness and courage they show for the liberation of the fatherland and of the greater Netherlands in the tropics.

Fellow-countrymen, I call on all of you who are liberated, and not least on the young, to prepare together with my ministers and myself the resurrection of the whole of the Netherlands territory and of the Netherlands East Indies, for I am convinced that thus we shall do all we can for our oppressed countrymen and the members of the empire.

Unite around your government, which will lead the way. And now, onward.

Long live the fatherland.

Long live the empire.

Circumstances had necessitated an execution in two stages of our original project, based on the assumption of a complete liberation, to form a cabinet of people who had spent the war in the Netherlands, immediately after the liberation. Or, to put it differently, part of the original plan had to be advanced.

A moment came when it was possible for King George to visit the Allied troops in our liberated south, whose headquarters were at Eindhoven. The news was the more interesting as it seemed to indicate that a short visit from me should also be possible in the near future. I had to proceed warily in this matter, so as to avoid the embarrassment of a reply to the effect that in the view of H.Q. the time had not yet come for me to visit the Netherlands. I had to put out a feeler before doing anything official. Fortunately this led to an assurance that an official request would be favourably received. The request followed at once: I asked to be allowed to pay a short visit to the three liberated provinces. Then we had to make our preparations, which of course took a little time.

Before I describe this tour there is something else I want to explain. Among the many people sent to London by Bernhard, to give information to me and to the ministers, there had been a Protestant and a Roman Catholic army chaplain of the B. S. The former arrived just as I began to prepare my tour, as if he had known about it.

I knew that I would meet prominent personages of the I. K. O. (Inter-Church Consultation) on my tour, including members of the provisional Synod of the Dutch Reformed Church. I was fully informed of the attitude of the churches towards the occupying power and of their co-operation; but from a distance I had not been able to acquire an inside understanding of the situation, after the radical changes that had occurred in the relations between the churches and in their approach to spiritual matters generally. My information had to be completed through conversations with people who stood at the heart of the nation's spiritual life. Reports alone were not sufficient; a living picture of the spiritual growth of the Netherlands could only come from personal contact. I derived great profit from the exploratory talks I had before I went and saw for myself.

To prepare my tour I had requests sent out to three personages, one in each province, to draw up a plan which should then be passed on to the G. H. Q. in our country; the Allied military authorities had to take the necessary measures, for there was one thing I should never forget: I was the guest of the authorities. Strange situation: to be on Dutch soil without ruling! The territory had not yet been transferred to the constitutional authorities. The Allied authorities discharged their task with admirable tact and hospitality; there was nothing strained about my return under their auspices.

As for my tour, it was different from any of my previous tours in its complete lack of luxury. I was accompanied by Baron Baud, my duaghter's private secretary, an ex-hostage of the Germans who had reported to her and whom she had put at my disposal for this occasion. He was made a colonel for the duration of the tour. For personal services I had a sergeant of my guard. Nobody else travelled with me, although Mrs. Verbrugge was with me at Anneville, the headquarters of the B. S. Our luggage was extremely restricted.

The programme for Zealand had been composed by Jonkheer de Casembroot, provincial deputy and former burgomaster of Westkapelle, a prominent member of the resistance. He and the Queen's Commissioner accompanied me in their province. The plan for Brabant was the work of Mr. Beel of Eindhoven, who had just been appointed Minister of the Interior. In his province, he and the acting Queen's Commissioner accompanied me, and in Limburg, the third of the southern provinces, my company was made up of Mr. Wijffels new Minister for Social Affairs who had prepared the programme, and the Queen's Commissioner.

The British military authorities had put a shell-proof car at my disposal and supplied us with army rations. Strict secrecy as regards the route we were to follow and the towns I would visit had been imposed upon ourselves as well as upon the British military authorities and all the Dutch people I was going to meet.

We arrived at the Dutch frontier near Eede on the morning of March 13th. I crossed it on foot.

After a moving welcome we drove on into the Netherlands. Wherever I went, the same emotion and enthusiasm. Everywhere flowers, presents and all sorts of attentions. In every town and village resistance workers and widows and children of fallen underground fighters were presented to me at my special request. I inspected all the units of the B. S. which were on duty on my way or which had been specially summoned to meet me; and I always spoke to some of the men. Officers of M. G. and civilian authorities reported in many places.

We made a long tour by car through Zealand Flanders, ending at Sluiskil. On the way we ate our rations at the home of Mr. Meijs, notary in Oostburg. The reader will easily understand the great joy it gave us to share them with our host and hostess.

We had dinner at the headquarters of the Dutch Naval Commander Southern Sector in Sluiskil, and we spent the night there. Early the next morning we set out on our tour of the eastern half of Zealand Flanders.

On the way we stopped near a bridge where the enemy had executed some of our boys not long before. I took the marguerite I wear on my coat and laid it at the spot where these heroes had fallen.

It is clearly impossible for me to mention all the places I visited; the reader will forgive me if I single out a few instances at random.

We visited Hulst and had our lunch at the old town hall. The resistance leaders present in the square outside were invited to join us with their wives. Fortunately the rations were ample and there was enough bread and coffee for everyone; the burgomaster treated us to apples from his garden. This meal was known as the heroes' luncheon.

After this visit I went to Anneville via Belgian territory. On Sunday I visited Breda and attended my first religious service in the Netherlands after five years.

On one of the following days I met a large group of dignitaries and private persons at Breda town hall. They included the Bishop of Breda,-- I always received the spiritual authorities--General Maczek, commanding the Polish division which had liberated Breda, and many resistance fighters and war victims.

Then back from Bréda to Zealand, where receptions of resistance fighters and war victims awaited me at Flushing and Middelburg.

The next day we left flooded Middelburg by 'DUKW' to visit Westkapelle and several villages on the way. I could now see for myself the catastrophic results Westkapelle had suffered from the bombing of the dike by the Allies. I was particularly affected by the account of a tragic drama in the mill: without any hope of assistance those inside it had watched the water mount higher and higher until in the end it carried them all away.

It was a cold, unforgettable journey. How tragic was the aspect offered by the Isle of Walcheren, once so picturesque: a surface of water as far as the eye could reach, with church spires and roofs rising out of it, and trees that would never put forth leaves again.

The next day we returned to Anneville, by way of Veere, Goes, Bergop-Zoom and Roosendaal. Everywhere the same emotion of the crowds who had flocked together, and meetings with resistance workers and widows and children of men who had given their lives for the great cause. My deepest feelings were always for them.

DOCUMENT XV

The Second World War left the Netherlands a shambles.
The following document, written in 1945, gives a good
impression of the bleak situation.

MEMORANDUM OF THE NETHERLANDS GOVERNMENT CONTAINING THE CLAIMS OF THE NETHERLANDS TO REPARATIONS FROM GERMANY

Provisional Statement

INTRODUCTION

1. The Netherlands Ministry for Foreign Affairs has the honour, in
compliance with an invitation sent by the Foreign Office to the Netherlands
Ambassador to the Court of St. James, dated August 27th 1945 No. UE
3812/3812/77, to transmit a memorandum containing the claims of the Netherlands to reparation from Germany.

2. In submitting these data the Netherlands Government would like to
make the following observations.

3. On more than one occasion, and lastly in a note addressed to the
Governments of the United Kingdom of Great Britain and Northern Ireland,
the United States of America, the Union of Socialist Soviet Republics and
France, dated August 17th 1945, the Netherlands Government have made it
known that in comparison with many other countries which suffered damage
in this war the country's economy suffered exceptionally as a result of
German aggression. For, although the position of the Netherlands until
September 1944 was in many respects comparable to that of other occupied
countries, after that date conditions deteriorated considerably. Consequently the Netherlands suffered more on account of the war than most, if
not all, other occupied European countries.

4. The liberation of the three Southern provinces of the Netherlands
and the gallant but abortive attempt to seize Arnhem, caused tremendous
and widespread destruction. In the eight provinces which continued to be
occupied by the Germans the enemy multiplied his predatory enterprises.
The worst looting in Holland took place in this last phase of the war in Europe. The contiguity of the Netherlands and Germany which are not sepa--
rated by an expanse of sea, made this easy. In some districts the country
was stripped completely bare, a fact which in Western Europe is believed
to be without precedent. In addition, more than eight percent of the agricultural area of the country was flooded, of which one half with sea water,
with all the long-term damage to the soil resulting therefrom. Moreover,
more than two percent of the total agricultural area was laid waste on ac-

count of the construction by the Germans of fortified zones, minefields and aerodromes, whilst another six percent have been rendered unfit for immediate use because of military operations. Considerable stretches of rich orchard country have been ruined for as long as it takes to grow fruit trees.

5. The case of the Netherlands is therefore exceptional and special.

6. The Netherlands Government are of the opinion that as an essential condition for the recovery of the country, and as a matter of plain justice, the people of the Netherlands have the undoubted right to the earliest possible restitution of all identifiable looted property taken from the country by the Germans, when such property is found outside the Netherlands, either in Germany or elsewhere. In the view of the Netherlands Government "looted property" includes all goods by their nature fit for restitution, which the enemy, his agents or his subjects, by favour of the occupation of the whole or of part of the Netherlands, have removed from the country's national patrimony as it existed before the occupation, either directly by acts of transfer or of dispossession, or indirectly by purchases or by transactions effected by means of payment which were created, imposed or extorted by the enemy due to the occupation. The Netherlands Government consider the restitution of looted property as a category per se which urgently demands special provisions.

It is a well established principle of law, that a person who discovers his property in the possession of another person, has the right to require its restitution, with priority over all creditors, and this, whether these creditors have an ordinary or a preferential claim. On page 1153 of the 7th edition of Thaller's "Traité élémentaire de droit commercial (1925)" this wellknown French jurist says (translated into English): "Every owner is armed with a jus in rem. The essential attribute of a jus in rem is its preferential character. Those who have a jus in rem are not subject to distribution on a pro rata basis. Their right takes precedence over all creditors."

The same principle prevails in Anglo-American law. According to paragraph 38 of the English Bankruptcy Act (1914) the right to claim restitution is denied the owner only in a few cases when the property in question has come into the possession of the creditor "by the consent and the permission of the true owner".[1]

For that reason J. W. Smith states in his "Compendium of Mercantile Law" (12th ed., p. 863): "The wrongful seizure of the goods by a wrongdoer would seem sufficient to take the goods out of the possession, order or disposition of the bankrupt".

The American Corpus Juris Secundum, the most modern compendium

---

1. Vide Williams, Law and Practice in Bankruptcy, 13th ed. p. 276, sq.

of United States law, recognizes a similar right of the owner[2] giving the same grounds as Thaller: "A reclamation proceeding in bankruptcy is in effect a proceeding in rem" (sub voce Bankruptcy, p. 940).

7. The damage done to the Netherlands by Germany far exceeds the removal by the Germans of property now to be restored in so far as it is still in existence and can be identified. In view thereof, the Netherlands Government furthermore insist on receiving a fair and equitable share of all German internal and external assets, to be used for reparation purposes, including usable industrial capital equipment, shares, or participations in enterprises, and all other German deliveries in kind, in gold, in foreign exchange, or in labour. All this with due regard to the exceptional position of the Netherlands as previously stated in this memorandum.

8. The Netherlands Government further recall that the Netherlands merchant navy has during five years of war taken an active part in the general allied war effort against Germany and Japan, and has given service second to none, suffering serious losses, which insofar as ships were concerned have been made good to an insignificant extent only. They therefore claim a fair and equitable share, both in regard to quantity and quality, of all vessels to be surrendered by Germany. This also applies to vessels destined for navigation on inland waterways, of which thousands belonging to the Netherlands were seized by the Germans during the war and subsequently destroyed.

9. With regard to the claims of the Netherlands to reparation from Germany, the following should be taken into account.

10. All data contained in the following pages are of a provisional nature. The central part of the Netherlands was liberated as recently as May 1945, little more than five months ago. In this interval it has not yet been possible to establish the necessary machinery for a complete enquiry concerning war damage. This memorandum contains the estimates which are now available. They have been drawn up with great care, so that it may be expected that the final data - which will be presented later - will not differ appreciably from the present figures. All detailed data available will be produced on request.

11. Insofar as damage to and loss of property is concerned, this memorandum covers the period from May 10th 1940 to May 7th 1945. Damage of this nature incurred since May 7th 1945 has not been included. Although such subsequent damage was actually done to Netherlands property, e.g. as a result of the clearing of German fortifications, this has not been taken into account, as in the opinion of the Netherlands Government a final date had to be chosen, for which V.E. Day was considered the most appropriate.

---

2. A claimant may maintain a petition in the bankruptcy court for the reclamation of identifiable property or its proceeds in the hands of the trustee in bankruptcy in which the petitioner claims an adverse interest or right of title (sub voce Bankruptcy, par. 264).

With regard to damage resulting from loss of production, this memorandum includes damage of this nature incurred after May 7th 1945, in addition to that incurred during the above mentioned period.

12. The Netherlands Government feel that in the final reparation account the damage should not be calculated in values existing at the time when the damage was inflicted, but in values providing full compensation (replacement values) at the time when the reparation account will be finally established. In order to comply with the desire expressed by the Governments concerned, the replacement values of 1938 have been provisionally taken as a basis. It should be borne in mind, however, that had the damage inflicted been expressed in terms of the price level now pervailing in the Netherlands, all figures mentioned in this memorandum would have had to be raised by 75%.

13. In compliance with the indications given with regard to the presentation of data concerning reparation claims, all values contained in this memorandum are expressed both in terms of Netherlands guilders and in terms of 1938 U.S. dollars, according to the average rate of exchange during that year, when $1. - equalled Fl. 1. 81 - 82.

14. Finally it should be made clear that in some paragraphs of this memorandum the Netherlands Government had to deviate from the required form of presentation on account of the insufficienty of data available.

EVALUATION OF DAMAGE CAUSED TO THE NETHERLANDS BY THE WAR AGAINST GERMANY

For practical reasons reparation will have to be restricted to damage capable of being expressed in terms of money. It comprises four categories:

A. material loss of the national wealth of the Netherlands;
B. damage owing to loss of production during the years of war;
C. loss owing to forced transfer to Germany of part of the reduced production;
D. damage owing to loss of production suffered and still to be suffered after May 7th 1945.

These four categories are not so distinct from one another as this enumeration might suggest. On more than one point they are interrelated, which entails the danger of double counting. In the following statement care has been taken to avoid such double countings.

Section I

A. Material loss of the national wealth of the Netherlands

This loss has been caused by destruction by or in consequence of direct acts of war, requisitions and looting by the occupying power, by the omission of normal replacement and maintenance of capital-goods, as well as by other forms of diminution of wealth (i.e. depletion of stocks in industry, agriculture, horticulture and trade, diminution of live-stock and of durable consumer goods).

 The loss on this account based on the price-level of 1938 is composed as follows:

a) direct damage owing to the war,
 the occupation and the evacua-
 tion . . . . £ 5 390 million or $ 2 965 million
b) damage on account of looting . . £ 3 640   " or $ 2 002 "
c) arrears in normal replacement
 and maintenance of capital-
 goods, as well as other forms of
 diminution of wealth . .. . £ 2 395   " or $ 1 3 17 "
        Total   11 425 million or $ 6 284 million

 This amount may be divided over the component parts of the national wealth as follows:

1. Industry, Commerce, Banking and Insurance: £4 015 million or $ 2 208 million.
 a. Industry: £2 200 million or $ 1 210 million,
 viz. damage to buildings and
  land . . . . £ 200 million or $ 110 million
  damage to machinery and
  plant . . . . £ 1000 " or $ 550 "
  damage to stocks . . . . . £ 1000 " or $ 550 "

 This damage includes an amount of £400 million or $ 220 million caused by the bombardment of Rotterdam and of a number of towns in the Southern and Eastern part of the country, as well as by other acts of war, an amount of £1 000 million or $ 550 million caused by requisitioning and looting by the occupying power of machinery, industrial plant and stocks of raw materials, semi-manufactured and manufactured goods and an amount of £800 million or $ 440 million on account of the omission of normal replacement and maintenance of industrial and commercial assets and diminution of stocks.

 b. Commerce: 1800 million or $990 million,
 viz. damage to shops, buildings,
  warehouses and plant . . . . £ 400 million or $ 220 million
  damage to stocks . . . . . . £ 1400 million or $ 770 "

 The above refers to war-damage to buildings, plant and loss of stocks to an amount of £500 million or $ 275 million, loss owing to requisitioning of supplies to an amount of £500 million or $ 275 million, as well as loss owing to the omission of normal replacement and maintenance of buildings and plant and diminution of supplies amounting to £800 million or $ 440 million.

At the outbreak of war total stocks available in industry and trade amounted to about £2 500 million or $ 1 350 million; at the end of the war these stocks had practically dwindled to nil. Considerable supplies of goods were lost by the bombardment of Rotterdam on May 14th 1940.

    c. <u>Banking</u> and <u>Insurance</u>: £15 million or $ 8 million.

This refers mainly to damage to buildings. The loss suffered by insurance companies is mentioned here pro memoria.

2. <u>Ocean</u> <u>shipping</u>, <u>Coastal</u> <u>shipping</u> <u>and</u> <u>Fisheries</u>: £325 million or $ 179 million,

    viz. damage to ships . . . . . . £ 300 million or $ 165 million
    damage to buildings . . . . . . £ 25 " or $ 14 "

About 50% of the Merchant Fleet was lost due to direct acts of war. The offices and plant on the wharves of the shipping companies also suffered considerable damage. Of the fishing fleet too, a considerable part was lost owing to acts of war.

3. <u>Harbours</u>, <u>harbour-works</u> <u>and</u> <u>port-installations</u>: £300 million or $165 million.

Apart from bombardments this damage was mainly a result of the destruction and blowing up of the harbour-works and plant in Rotterdam. Amsterdam and along the larger rivers by the occupying power.

4. <u>Means</u> <u>of</u> <u>Transport</u>: £680 million or $ 374 million,

    viz. damage to Railways . . . . . £ 300 million or $ 165 million
         damage to Tramways . . . . £ 30 " or $ 16.5 "
         damage to Inland fleet . . . £ 100 " or $ 55 "
         damage to Civil air fleet . . £ 10 " or $ 5.5 "
         damage to Road vehicles
         (lorries), etc. . . . . £ 240 " or $ 132 "

Damage to these catagories amounting to £240 million or $ 132 million was caused by direct acts of war. The rest, amounting to £440 million or $ 242 million, refers almost entirely to loss due to requisitioning and looting by the occupying power. For instance nearly the entire rollingstock of Railways was carried off, whilst a very great number of trams, omnibuses, lorries, motorcars and other means of transport by land or water were lost owing to looting.

5. <u>Roads</u>, <u>including</u> <u>bridges</u>: £100 million or $55 million.

The damage to bridges has, apart from direct acts of war, chiefly been due to destruction and blowing up by the occupying power. The damage to roads is stated under 7.

6. <u>Agriculture</u>, <u>horticulture</u> <u>and</u> <u>forestry</u>: £825 million or $454 million,

    viz. damage to buildings and territory . . . .£500 million or $ 275 million

damage to machinery, imple-
ments and stocks . . . . .   £ 75 million or $ 41.5 million
damage to live-stock . . .   £ 250   "   or $ 137.5   "

Damage of this category amounting to £400 million or $220 million
is due to direct acts of war, the construction of aerodromes and fortifications, evacuation, inundations (this includes an amount of £130 million
or $ 71.5 million on account of the inundation of the Isle of Walcheren);
£100 million or $ 55 million owing to requisitioning of supplies, agricultur-
al implements and part of the live-stock, and £325 million or $ 179 million
owing to the omission of normal maintenance of buildings and of agricultural implements and owing to decrease of supplies and live-stock.
     In course of time data concerning the period during which the land in
question has been or will be unproductive owing to acts of war, will be submitted.

7. Public property: £150 million or $ 82.5 million.
     Owing to the fact that no detailed data concerning damage to public
undertakings are yet available, this damage has been stated provisionally
under damage to Industry (see above under 1). Damage to harbours, har-
bourworks, etc., in as much as these are public property, has been stated
under 3. Further damage to public property refers to damage to aerodromes, buildings, schools, roads, waterways, sewerage, etc.

8. Household articles and personal effects: £1 200 million or $ 660 million.
     The contents of a very great number of houses have been destroyed
or heavily damaged as a result of acts of war. Damage on that account is
estimated at £700 million or $385 million. Moreover, about 600 000 wire-
less sets and 1 000 000 bicycles were requisitioned by the Germans and
the furniture of numerous Jews and other persons was confiscated. Damage on this account amounts to roughly £150 million or $ 82.5 million.
Furthermore the loss owing to omission of the necessary maintenance
and replacement of non-perishable consumer goods is estimated at £350
million or $ 193 million.

9. Gold and foreign exchange, foreign investments and valuables: £2 850
     million or $1 567 million.
     a. Gold and foreign exchange: £1 210 million or $ 665 million.
     This item refers to gold of the Netherlands Bank amounting to £292
million or $ 161 million, carried off by the occupying power, as well as
to foreign banknotes amounting to £14 million or $ 7.7 million and to sil-
ver, nickel and bronze coin seized to an amount of £4 million or $ 2.2 mil-
lion. It should further be taken into account that the Netherlands National
Wealth suffered a loss of about £900 million or $ 495 million in consequence
of war-expenditure incurred by the Netherlands Government in London, in
so far as this took the form of disposing of part of the Netherlands gold-

reserve abroad, of Netherlands balances in foreign countries, as well as
of commitments entered into in foreign countries.

    b. Foreign investments: £1000 million or $ 550 million.

    An amount of £500 million or $ 275 million refers to German and
other foreign securities which the Germans obtained in this country by con-
fiscating Jewish and other Dutch property, whilst damage amounting to
£500 million or $ 275 million arose from loss of Netherlands investments
in Central Europe in consequence of the war.

    c. Valuables (carried off by the German occupying power): £ 640 million
        or $ 352 million,

viz.				
jewelry	£300 million	or	$ 165 million	
rough diamonds	£ 34.5 "	or	$ 19 "	
silver and gold objects	£ 5 "	or	$ 2.75 million	
platinum	£ 0.5 "	or	$ 0.275 "	
pictures..................	£200 "	or	$ 110 "	
objects of a scientific nature	£50 "	or	$ 27 "	
objects of an educational na-				
ture......................	£ 50 "	or	$ 27 "	

10. Houses and buildings not otherwise included: £970 million or $533.5
     million.

    a. Houses: £820 million or $ 451 million.

    100 000 houses have been entirely destroyed, 50 000 have been heavi-
ly damaged and 300 000 have been damaged by direct acts of war, by demolition in the coastal zone or as a result of evacuation. The damage on that
account amounts to a total of £700 million or $ 385 million. The loss
owing to the omission of maintenance and replacement is estimated at
£120 million or $ 66 million.

    b. Churches, private nursing-homes, schools, buildings belonging to
        societies and associations, theatres, cinemas, etc.: £150 million
        or $ 82.5 million.

    This mainly refers to direct war-damage and damage due to demoli-
tions in the coastal zone.

11. Other material damage and loss.
    Property pertaining to the liberal professions: £10 million or $ 5.5
    million.

    The table printed at the end of this memorandum gives a survey of
the Netherlands National Wealth on September 1st 1939 and its decline owing
to the war in conformity with the above enumeration, based on the values
of 1938. Furthermore, it is pointed out that the damage referred to on page
208 under B, C, and D has been stated under Section III.

Section I I

Budgetary expenditures allocatable to the war against Germany

The expenditure of the Netherlands Government on account of the conduct of the war agai nst Germany amounts to £1 600 million or $ 880 million, viz. £700 million or $ 385 million on account of expenses of mobilization before May 10th 1940 and £900 million or $ 495 million on account of war-expenditure of the Netherlands Government in London. In order to avoid this latter item being counted twice, it is recalled that this expenditure has already been included in Section I.

Section III

Man-years lost through the war against Germany

An exact statement of the number of man-years lost on account of the war-effort of the Netherlands against Germany owing to deportation of Netherlands subjects to Germany and to forced labour performed in behalf of the occupying power, cannot yet be submitted. This also applies to loss of life and to the number of sick and wounded. Data referring thereto will be supplied later.

Nevertheless a rough estimate may now be given of the damage incurred by these losses. In this connection reference is made to the categories of damage stated under B, C, and D on page 10, concerning which the following observations may now be made.

B.   Damage owing to loss of production during the years of war

Instead of loss of production it is also possible to speak of a dimunition of the national income. The various causes underlying the fact that the total national income during the period from May 10th 1940 to May 7th 1945 was lower than was normal before the war are discussed below.

An indication of the decline in production during the years from 1940 to 1944 is given by the following general index of the production of goods and services composed by the Central Bureau of Statistics at The Hague.

General index of agricultural and industrial production and of services rendered from 1938-1944.

1938 - 100	1941 - 91	1944 - 60.
1939 - 108	1942 - 80	
1940 - 99	1943 - 72	

On the basis of these index-numbers the Central Bureau of Statistics has calculated that the real national income, i.e. the national income expressed in terms of goods available for consumption and investment, has throughout the period of war been at least £6 000 million or $ 3 300 million lower than it would have been if production could have been maintained at the level of 1938. The amount of £6 000 million or $ 3 300 million has been based on the price level of 1938.

It should be remarked that the index-numbers used are mainly based on data concerning the extent of the production. The decline in quality of the production resulting from the consumption of substitutes and from poorer methods of production could not be taken into sufficient account. This

is one of the reasons why the amount mentioned as £6 000 million or
$ 3 300 million may be considered as being rather low.

On the other hand it should be observed that it would not be right to
add the total decline of the national income during the years of occupation
as second loss to the amount of the loss of material wealth. This may best
be shown by an examination of the causes to which loss of production during
the years of war is to be attributed. These causes are the following:

1. The change in the international position of the Netherlands. Owing
to the fact that Germany made war on the Netherlands, the supply of raw
materials and auxiliary materials for industry and agriculture from overseas was stopped. The diminution of the national income which thus became inevitable, was further hastened and aggravated by the fact that Germany seized the greater part of the supplies. The direct loss caused by
stocks being carried off, has been mentioned in Section I; the effect of this
removal on the extent of the national income will be discussed below under
4. It may be stated here that the looting of raw materials etc. by the Germans can be no reason not to consider the change of the international position of the Netherlands due to the country's occupation as an independent
cause of the decline of the national income. The reduction of the national
income resulting from this cause should be fully charged to Germany's account.

2. The dislocation of Holland's economic policy becoming apparent
from the fact that the historically-grown equilibrium of the country's industrial life has been upset and from the smaller "productiveness" of the government apparatus, etc. The diminution of the national income resulting
from this cause, should be fully charged to Germany's account.

3. The working-power of the Netherlands nation as affected not only by
murder, imprisonment or deportation to Germany of civilians, but also by
civilians being bodily or mentally mutilated in the war or made victims of
the insufficient food position, and by the death of members of the armed
forces and of the merchant navy and of those fallen in the struggle put up
by the resistance groups, etc. The diminution of the national income resulting from this cause should be fully charged to the account of Germany.

4. War-damage of a material nature. The loss of production caused
during the war by damage of this kind should not be added in full to other
forms of war-damage if double counting is to be avoided.

The capital goods employed in production derive their value from
their total contribution to the ultimate product, i.e. to the national income.
In the normal course of events there is on the one hand this contribution,
whilst on the other hand the supply of capital goods is kept up to the mark
by replacement and maintenance, charged against the national income.

During the occupation both these features had to be neglected. As
neither replacement nor maintenance took place, loss of wealth was incurred; this loss of £1 000 million or $ 550 million was entered under the
heading of material damage. On the other hand, the omission of replacement and maintenance also meant that production for purposes of replacement and maintenance could not take place, so that the national income de-

creased to an amount equal to the loss already taken into account. This part of the toal diminution of the national income should therefore not once again be counted as war-damage.

A similar reasoning holds good with regard to capital-goods lost owing to the use of force or in consequence of requisitioning in behalf of the enemy. Thus the whole contribution was lost which these capital-goods would have made to the national income during the occupation, and partly even for many years to come. The capitalized value of this contribution was included in Section I. The part of the total diminution of the national income resulting directly from the loss of this contribution may therefore not be counted once again as war damage. It may be calculated at the full value of the supplies of raw materials carried off or destroyed (£900 million or $ 495 million) and at part of the value of the factory-buildings etc. destroyed and of the machinery etc. carried off (£100 million or $ 55 million).

Ultimately, therefore, the amount of loss of production during the years of war which, in addition to the material war-damage, has to be charged to the account of Germany amounts to £4 000 million or $ 2 200 million.

Of course it would also be possible to find this amount if all component items could be stated singly. This is only possible in a few exceptional cases. One of these is the wellknown railway-strike, which by order of the Netherlands Government in London set in on September 17th 1944. The loss incurred during the period of this strike is the equivalent of the amount normally required during such a period for purchasing coal etc., for paying wages and salaries, for the interest of the capital invested and for depreciation. This amount may be fixed at £100 million or $ 55 million.

In order to give an idea of the importance of the loss of production involved it may finally be stated that the national income for 1938 is to be estimated at £5 100 million or $ 2 800 million, not including the proceeds of investments in the Netherlands-Indies and in foreign countires.

C. Loss owing to forced transfer to Germany of part of the reduced pro-
    duction

The loss of production as calculated sub B is not the only form of loss suffered by the national income during the period of occupation. A considerable part of what was produced had to be put at the disposal of the occupying power or was exported to Germany and other countries, without a balance in the form of an equivalent payment in goods. This production in behalf of the occupying power is expressed on the money-side in the cost of the occupation and in the enormous increase of the balance of Reichsmark of the Netherlands Bank. The expenses on occupation-account are calculated, including the so-called "äussere Besatzungskosten", at a total of 9 500 million guilders or 5 225 million dollars, while the Reichsmark-claim of the Netherlands Bank had ultimately risen to £4 500 million or $ 2 475 million. This latter amount would be very considerably larger, if the expenses on occupation-account had not repeatedly been "recovered" by writing off from the Reichsmark account of the Netherlands Bank. The Netherlands Government had to refund to the Bank the amounts written off. so that consequently the amount of the cost of the occupation was correspondingly increased.

The total amount of the cost of occupation and of the Reichsmark-balance of the Netherlands Bank does not, however, exclusively consist of the countervalue of goods and services withdrawn from current production. The cost of occupation also includes amounts for the transfer of immovables and other property. As regards the claims of the Netherlands Bank, these did not only arise from the exportation of goods produced in the Netherlands, but also because Dutch, German, Hungarian and other securities, the property of Netherlands subjects, were compulsorily sold abroad in large numbers, and furthermore because labourers deported to Germany transferred wages to the Netherlands. On the other hand, however, the cost of the occupation does not comprise all supplies and services in behalf of the German occupation, because all sorts of expenses were charged by order of the occupying power directly to the account of the Public Treasury. The expenses just referred to amount to a round sum of 250 million or $ 137 million. It should be emphatically stated in this connection that this amount does not refer to damage to property in consequence of the occupation. The said amount comprises items such as transport-services never paid for by the occupying power (e.g. the transport of German forces by the Netherlands Railways), unpaid rent of buildings seized by the occupying power, trading-losses and inevitable expenses resulting from measures of occupation. As was stated above, these items were charged directly to the account of the Public Treasure by order of the occupying power and have therefore not been entered under the heading "cost of occupation".

With the help of the available figures on the returns of production and exportation the Central Bureau of Statistics has calculated that Germany had to her disposal a net amount of £6, 000 million of $ 3 300 million of the current production of goods and services throughout the entire period of occupation, which amount was therefore withdrawn from the Netherlands national income. This calculation is based on the prices of 1938.

D. Damage owing to loss of production suffered and still to be suffered after May 7th 1945

The chaotic condition, in which the country's economy has been left at the end of the war, is the reason that for some years to come we shall have to reckon with a greatly reduced real income. This is a result of damage done to the production-apparatus by the war and by the occupation and of damage inflicted to the productivity of labour by all kinds of psychic and physical factors. Detrimental consequences of imprisonment and forced employment in Germany, undernourishment, decline of the general state of public health, lack of workingclothes and footwear, insufficient housing, defective means of conveyance, bad equipment of factories and workshops, shortage of the most essential tools and auxiliary materials, are the principal causes of the now greatly decreased labour-productivity. Reconstruction will proceed but slowly, since it depends on how soon the most urgent shortages can be supplemented by imports from abroad and the most necessary repairs can be carried out.

Assuming that the labour-productivity at the end of the war amounted to 40% of the normal (the average of 1938), that from July 1st 1945 it increased regularly and that on account of this increase it will be 100% again at the close of 1947, one arrives at the conclusion that the loss owing to the decreased labour-productivity may be fixed at 85% of a normal net annual production. Taking the latter at approximately £5 500 million or $ 3 025 million, the loss for this item alone, based on the purchasing-power of the money of 1938, is £4 700 million or $ 2 585 million.

Just as with the loss sub B, some double counting has to be rectified. The amount involved is, however, not so considerable as in the case of the calculation of the loss of production during the years of occupation, since replacement and maintenance will be proceeding again and since no deduction is necessary for the large supplies of raw materials and auxiliary materials lost in the years of war. In connection with the fact that loss owing to the destruction of factories, etc. has already been entirely booked under Section I, in this case a deduction must take place. It seems right in view of the foregoing to fix the amount to be charged to Germany owing to loss of production suffered and still to be suffered after May 7th 1945, at £4 300 million or $ 2 364 million. In this case too, it should in theory be possible to calculate the total by adding up all items in which the future, loss of production is concretely expressed. In practice, however, this is only possible in a few exceptional cases.

Section IV
Cost of German occupation

The cost of German occupation amounts to a total of £9 500 million or $ 5 224 million,

viz. Reichskreditkassenscheine......£   135 million or $ 74 million
Expenses of German Forces[1] .. £ 7 030   "   or $ 3 866   "
Expenses of German Civil Administration..................£   225   "   or $ 124   "
Compulsory Contributions to the cost of Germany's war against Russia...................... £ 2 110   "   or $ 1 160   "

Total   £ 9 500 million or $5 224 million

---

1. These do not include the cost of occupation charged directly to the Public Treasury by order of the occupying power. On page 215 the amount of these expenses, not including the damage to goods mentioned in Section I, is calculated at £250 million or $ 137 million.

GERMAN INTERESTS IN THE NETHERLANDS IMMEDIATELY BEFORE THE WAR

The data to be supplied with regard to German interests in the Netherlands immediately before the war, cannot yet be furnished, as these interests are to a large extent concentrated in the central part of the Netherlands, which was only liberated by the Allies in May 1945, so that the time has been too short to collect sufficient information. However, it may be noted that a separate institution has been created for the registration and the administration of German interests. As soon as more detailed data are obtained, they will be made available, together with a survey of the way in which these interests are administered. Nevertheless, it can now already be stated that before the war the value of these interests was estimated at £1 000 million of $ 550 million. Considerable war-damage to these interests will, however, have to be taken into account. In this connection it should be observed that against these pre-war German interests in the Netherlands there exists the item of the not inconsiderable Netherlands interests in Germany, which before the war were estimated at £1 500 million of $ 825 million; here too, however, a considerable war-damage will have to be taken into account, a war-damage which has only partly been entered under the heading: Foreign investments, included in Section I.

SUMMARY

In view of the above the total amount which the Netherlands Government have decided to claim from Germany as reparation for war-damage suffered, can, expressed in the money-value of 1938, be fixed as follows:

A. Material loss of the national
   wealth of the Netherlands....... £ 11 425 million or $ 6 284 million
B. Damage owing to loss of produc-
   tion during the years of war.... £ 4 000   "   or $ 2 200   "
C. Loss owing to forced transfer to
   Germany of part of the reduced
   production................... £ 6 000   "   or $ 3 300   "
D. Damage owing to loss of produc-
   tion suffered and still to be suf-
   fered after May 7th 1945........ £ 4 300   "   or $ 2 364   "

£ 25 725 million or $14 148 million.

THE NATIONAL WEALTH OF THE NETHERLANDS ON SEPTEMBER 1ST 1939 AND ITS DECLINE IN CONSEQUENCE OF THE WAR

(All data have been based on the pricelevel of 1938)

	Property on September 1st 1939 in millions	Decline owing to the war in millions
a. Agriculture and horticulture.....	£ 3 800 or $ 2 090	£825 or $ 454
b. Industry	£ 5 000 or $ 2 750	£2 200 or $ 1 210
c. Commerce....................	£ 2 500 or $ 1 375	£1 800 or $ 990
d. Credits and Banking...........	£ 300 or $ 165	£15 or 8
e. Traffic......................	£ 1 500 or $ 825	£1 005 or 553
f. Public property (incl. harbours and bridges, excl. utilities).....	£ 2 800 or $ 1 540	£550 or $ 303
g. Churches, private nursinghomes, buildings belonging to private institutions, theatres, cinemas....	£500 or $ 275	£150 or $ 82, 5
h. Liberal professions (inventories).	£ 50 or $ 27	£10 or $ 5, 5
i. Houses.......................	£5 000 or $ 2 750	£820 or $ 451
j. Furniture.....................	£5 000 or $ 2 750	£1 200 or $ 660
k. Gold-stock and foreign exchange.	£1 500 or $ 825	£1 210 or $ 665
l. Investments in the Neth. Indies and abroad...................	£7 000 or $ 3 850	£1 000 or $ 550[2]
m. Valuables....................	£ 1	£ 640 or $ 352

Total national wealth:	Total damage:
£ 34 950 or $19 222	£ 11 425 or $ 6 284

As has already been observed in the beginning of this memorandum, this amount will in course of time have to be expressed in terms of the price-level prevailing at the time of the final settlement of the reparation account. At the present price-level (175% of that of December 31st 1938) the total damage incurred would not amount to £25 725 million of $14 148 million ($ 1.-- = £1.81 ~ 82, rate of exchange 1938) but to approximately £45 000 million or approximately $ 16 850 million, taking into account the present exchange rate of the guilder (i.e. 1 $ = £2.67).

---

1. Sufficient information is not available, but will be supplied at an early date.
2. The amount of £1000 million entered as loss on foreign investments only covers the loss on investments in the Central-European countries and the loss owing to confiscation of foreign securities belonging to Jewish and other Netherlands subjects. The loss on investments in the Netherlands Indies is therefore not included in this figure of £1 000 million.

DOCUMENT XVI

The Indonesian Problem

a.   After the German capitulation the Dutch Government began to prepare the military operations to recapture the Netherlands Indies. The following document is a letter from Lieutenant Governor-General Hubert van Mook to Admiral Sir James Somerville, the British member of the Combined Chiefs of Staff in Washington.

San Francisco, May 29, 1945

My Dear Admiral,

Although our conversation on Saturday night left me with considerable doubts about a speedy and helpful decision with regard to our pressing needs for transport, I also got the impression that you wanted to judge our position as fairly as possible. I think, therefore, that I should try to put that position before you in writing as I see it, and as, to my conviction, our people both in Holland and in the Indies will see it when they can review all the facts.

I have no quarrel with the grand strategy of going as directly as possible for the heart of the enemy. I must contend, however, that in the choice between the lines of approach, the nature and the allegiance of the countries, through which they pass, always play a part, For instance, the advance towards the Philippines might have been made through the Moluccas instead of through the jungle of New Guinea, but as the Australians had an excellent fighting force available, I can see how that may have had its influence on the initial choice of direction.

If we accept this overall strategy, however, the fact remains that its conception and execution have been and are extremely unfortunate, both for the European and for the Asiatic part of our Kingdom. The most important part of Holland was cut off and left in the hands of a desperate foe up to the very end of the war with Germany. The Netherlands Indies are being cut off and probably will be left in the hands of an equally desperate foe long after the Philippines, Burma, Malaya and maybe even French Indo-China shall have been liberated.

It will take some explaining to the common people in the Netherlands and the Indies that this had to be and that it was not merely a consequence of our own weakness in armed forces. Again I can quite understand that, apart from grand strategy, it was natural for the Americans to liberate the whole of the Philippines before going on, as it is natural for the Australians to clear the Solomons, New Britain and North East New Guinea, and as it will be natural for you to want to clear the whole of Burma and Malaya. Our people will not begrudge the more fortunate inhabitants of those countries their early freedom, although their own fate becomes more atrocious with every month of prolonged captivity.

But it will inevitably increase their desire, now that they are free again, to rearm as quickly as possible, to take part in the war and to help in speeding up the liberation of their compatriots, who are still under occupation of the enemy. No amount of grand stategy can explain why this should be delayed. We have not husbanded our forces when they were few and scattered, but we have a right to assistance in building them up again now that we have regained access to part of our manpower. Our allies would have a right to criticize us if we did _not_ want to do our utmost now; they have no right to refuse the comparatively slight assistance we ask of them to enable us to increase our participation in a war, which we declared when they were attacked.

The argument about preferring trained troops to troops still to be trained surely does not hold. The Americans and yourselves are still training new draftees, and you and we are training native auxiliaries in the liberated areas of the Far East. The French are training troops for the war against Japan and it would be bitter irony of they could do in Indo-China, which was surrendered without a fight, what would be denied to us in the Netherlands Indies, which resisted the Japanese ever since 1940.

During our conversation, the word prestige was used. If its use implied that our requests were only based on prestige and the prestige should not count, both implications would be grossly unfair. There are much more potent reasons for our request: I shall go into them presently. But the British, of all people, should know that prestige is not a negligible factor and least of all in the Orient. American prestige was certainly not unconnected with the Philippine campaign: your prestige plays its part in the drive for Burma and Malaya. I shall not try to guess in how far prestige has to do with the determination of the relative share in the war against Japan of British, American and Australian forces. But even the ordinary desire to hit back when you have been hit cannot be put aside, if the decent peoples of this world are going to survive against the gangsters. And we owe it to our people in the Indies that we do not sit at the ringside watching how others beat the Jap. It is, of course, pleasant if you are in a position to combine prestige with grand stategy, but even if that is not quite possible, a certain urge to get our own back has a right to enter as an element into our policy.

There was also mentioned the fact that we are a small nation. We have heard that before. But we cannot see how it can be of any advantage either to ourselves or to our allies or to the world to draw the conclusion that because of our smallness we should remain unarmed or abstain from fighting the enemy. We also happen to be a proud nation and, small in numbers though we be, it seems to me an asset to our friends if that pride is maintained. And just at this moment it is of vital importance for our people, after an unarmed resistance of five bitter years, to have the opportunity of fighting our enemies in a more regular war. If they are frustrated in that desire, because their help is deemed too insignificant, they will be led to the conclusion that their resistance during the years of occupation is equally underrated.

I do not think that you would like to see small nations like ours reduced to some sort of civilized helotism, because that would seriously weaken the community of really peace loving, decent nations, including the British Commonwealth.

I have given you two psychological reasons for assisting the Netherlands in their desire to rearm, which may seem "political" to a fighting sailor. But I don't think they can be neglected, especially not in the face of the great and enthusiastic response our call for volunteers has elicited from the first moment of liberation. It is worth while to sustain this spirit: it is dangerous, both for our country and for its friends and neighbours to undermine it. I think you had a similar experience when the United States extended the help of lend lease to you in your hour of need. When we ask for assistance we do it in the same spirit as you did then.

But I shall now give two more direct reasons for providing this assistance.

This war has two objectives: to defeat the enemy and to do so at the lowest cost. I think I need not prove that we are in this war as a whole: not just with a narrow view on our direct interests. But this does not mean that we can neglect those interests. We want to take part, if possible in the drive against Japan; but we want very much also to liberate our people in the Indies, Netherlanders and Indonesians, as quickly and with as little prolongation of their misery as possible. We probably haven't got the time nor, maybe, the force to do this all by ourselves. Moreover we forsee that our allies, you and the Americans and the Australians, will come to ask us to take a greater part, especially in the tedious and bloody mopping up that may follow the capture of the main enemy positions. We are eager to do so, but we cannot do it without adequate and timely preparation. Our participation will spare many allied lives, as it will save many of the lives of Her Majesty's subjects.

If -- as we hoped -- training of the first thousands could have started in January of this year, we might even now have been in a position to liberate a considerable number of islands in the Eastern part of the Indies, which are but weakly held, and so relieve the terror reigning there. We might even have been able to take over and hold the positions in New Guinea recently evacuated by the Americans and reoccupied by the Japanese, who will now have to be ejected again with considerable loss of lives.

You cannot put against this argument any guarantee that this will be done by your or other allied troops. You have to reckon, as we have, with public opinion at home that will want to see your soldiers and sailors return once Japan herself is beaten. But you know as well as I do that the surrender of Japan proper will most probably not mean the surrender of all her troops in the occupied areas.

But while we cannot be content with the contemptible role of goose-stepping in after others have done the fighting, we might not even be able to do that if the delays in training and transporting our men from Holland continue. Even for that job we need trained men brought to the spot; up till now we haven't got them and we cannot yet see when we are going to get them. If Japan should surrender before we have them, and if her troops should pull out of certain important areas, or if an expedition to one of the major islands should be launched, we would have to ask you, or the Americans, or the Australians not only to leave an armed force in occupation but also to take over the government and to take care of relief and rehabilitation for the time being. This is literally true. And although you were inclined to make light of such a situation with regard to its effects for us, I refuse to believe that you could possibly mean that seriously. I can only say that no Netherlands Government could accept responsibility for it and live.

Although I would not like to pretend that we got no help at all in the matter, I cannot but observe that there has been but slow progress and that the objections have been more frequent than the suggestions. It took over two months to convince S.H.A.E.F. and twenty-one Army Group that part of the volunteers in the Southern Netherlands could be assigned for duties overseas right away. When this was decided, the matter of transport took another month. At one time there were no uniforms, even for a few hundred men. The transport to Australia of 5600 men, promised on the 16th of April until the end of the war in Europe, did not materialize and has now been reduced to a paltry 600. There is as yet no arrangement in England for alternative training; there are neither facilities nor food in Holland for that purpose. The Australian army was very helpful and agreed to put at our disposal camps, equipment and training facilities in Western Austraila, which were ideally suited for the training of the light batallions we shall need; but they wanted us to take over those camps within a reasonable time. Because we obtained no transport, this offer threatened to lapse, entailing further unpredictable delays. We organized with great exertion and in the face of almost unsurmountable difficulties a Netherlands Indies Government center in Brisbane, where we could handle the executive business for the liberated areas, the problems of relief and rehabilitation, and the training of badly needed civil affairs people at the same time. I think we did a good job with almost no personnel, but now there are hundreds of indispensable men and women in the Netherlands, and in England, twiddling their thumbs, becoming rebellious and discouraged because they cannot be transported. Meanwhile the theatre commanders ask us where those people we promised them are, and begin to doubt our capacity and our good faith.

The only parts of the program that have reached a certain stage of execution are the training of an initial group of our marines in the U.S.A. (about 15% of the total), of a few hundred officers and N.C.O.'s in England and of some naval personnel in the same country. Otherwise things are at

a standstill. We cannot possibly go on like this. We ask for positive assistance; not for reasons why the plans which were approved by the C.C.O.
S. cannot be executed.

And, finally, I want to emphasize again that we are not asking much
outside assistance; much less as a matter of fact that many others who got
more help. For transport we ask the use of a few of our own ships. Indeed, we cannot produce equipment but up till now we have largely paid
ourselves for what we needed, either in cash or in a reverse lend lease or
in mutual aid. We want to handle our own relief and our own civil affairs
problems.

This then, my dear Admiral, is the position. It is a dangerous position. We can no longer pretend, either towards the Commanders in Chief,
or toward the Netherlands and the Indonesian people, that we shall be able
to do in the Indies what is expected, even demanded of us. But we shall
have to explain why. We do not want to do so because it will created justified disappointment and bad feeling, where bad feeling should not exist or
arise. But we cannot go on carrying a responsibility which is not ours to
carry.

I told you that one of the main themes of Japanese propaganda in the
Indies during the last year has been the absence of Dutch fighting forces
in the war against them. This kind of propaganda must have its influence,
in the long run, if the facts seem to confirm its truth. If it could apply to
your own case, you would strain every effort to remedy the situation. I
think that you can understand why we cannot acquiesce in a position, which
makes it impossible for us to get our men to the point in time.

You may be of opinion that, however true and cogent all this may
be, it is your duty to view things from a purely military point of view and
that from that point of view other things should have precedence. I have
already stated why I think that even purely military considerations support
our request because the availability of trained Netherland forces for the
mopping up in the Indies will spare British and American lives, will hasten
the process of their liberation, and will prevent an increased chaos and destruction. But apart from that military decisions inevitably have political
consequences. And if these consequences are deemed fatal to the future
of a country, the Government of that country cannot be asked to accept
them.

I hope that this letter may contribute to a better understanding of
our problem and to its speedy solution. I am sure that you will see why
we cannot treat the matter lightly, and I would like to expect that we shall
get your help in the approval of our request.

Yours sincerely

H.J. VAN MOOK.

b. The discussions between Indonesian nationalist leaders and the
Netherlands Government about Indonesian independence were broken off in
the summer of 1947 by Dutch military action. The United Nations inter-
vened and offered its "good offices," which led in January 31, 1948 to the
following agreement signed on neutral territory aboard the U.S. ship Renville.   The agreement implied the formation of a Federal State of Indonesia of which the Republic of Indonesia on Java would be a member. The
Dutch immediately went ahead with the creation of a provisional federal
government. Growing tension between the Dutch and the leaders of the
Republic led to a new Dutch military action in December, 1948, and intervention of the Security Council of the United Nations.

"(1) Sovereignty throughout the Netherlands Indies is and shall remain with the Kingdom of the Netherlands until, after a stated interval, the
Kingdom transfers its sovereignty to the United States of Indonesia. Prior
to the termination of such interval, the Kingdom may confer appropriate
rights, duties, and responsibilities on a Provisional Federal Government
of the territories of the future United States of Indonesia. The U.S.I.,
when created, will be a sovereign and independent State in equal partner-
ship with the Kingdom in a Netherlands-Indonesian Union, at the head of
which shall be the King (Queen) of the Netherlands. The status of the Republic of Indonesia will be that of a State within the United States of Indonesia.

(2) In any Provisional Federal Government created prior to the ratification of the future Constituion of the U.S.I., all States will be offered
fair representation.

(3) Either party may request that the services of the Committee of
Good Offices be continued to assist in adjusting differences between the
parties which may arise during the interim period. The other party will
oppose no objection to such a request, which would be brought to the attention of the Security Council by the Netherlands Government.

(4) Within 6-12 months of the signing of the present agreement, a
plebiscite will be held to determine whether the populations of the various
territories of Java, Madura, and Sumatra wish to form part of the Republic of Indonesia or of another State within the United States of Indonesia.
Such plebicite is to be conducted under observation by the Committee of
Good Offices, should either party request the services of the Committee
in this capacity. The parties may agree that another method for ascertain-
ing the will of the populations may be employed in place of a plebiscite.

(5) Following the delineation of the States in accordance with the
procedure set forth in (4) above, a Constitutional Convention will be con-
vened, through democratic procedures, to draft a Constitution for the
United States of Indonesia. The representation of the various States in the
Convention will be in proportion to their populations.

(6) Should any State decide not to ratify the Constitution, and desire, in accordance with the principles of the Linggadjati Agreement (see

8272 A), to negotiate a special relationship with the United States of Indonesia and the Kingdom of the Netherlands, neither party will object.

(7) Provision shall be made for a suitable period, not less than 6 months nor more than a year after the signing of the agreement, during which time uncoerced discussion and consideration of vital issues will proceed. At the end of this period free elections will be held for self-determination by the people of their political relationship to the United States of Indonesia.

(8) If, after signing the Agreement, either party should ask the U.N. to provide an agency to observe conditions at any time up to the point at which sovereignty is transferred from the Netherlands Government to the United States of Indonesia, the other party will take this request into serious consideration."

(9)-(12) These principles were taken from the Linggadjati Agreement, and provided for independence for the Indonesian peoples; co-operation between the peoples of the Netherlands and Indonesia; a reaffirmation that democratic processes would be employed in setting up the proposed Indonesian State on a federal basis; and the creation of a union between the Kingdom of the Netherlands and the United States of Indonesia under the Netherlands Sovereign.

The truce agreement signed on the Renville comprised the following nine points:

(1) Both parties to issue cease-fire orders to their forces simultaneously.

(2) The new status quo line to be the "van Mook line" of Aug. 29, 1947, with a demilitarized zone between the Dutch and Indonesian positions.

(3) The status quo line to be of a provisional character, without impairing the rights or claims of either party.

(4) The U.N. to place military observers at the disposal of both parties.

(5) Pending a political settlement, a civil police force to be responsible for maintaining law and order in the demilitarized zone.

(6) Trading and economic exchanges between the Dutch and Indonesian-controlled areas to be resumed as soon as possible.

(7) Hostile propaganda, as well as the publication of military communiqués, to cease on both sides.

(8) Republican troops in West Java to be withdrawn behind the status quo line.

(9) The agreement to be binding until one of the parties informs the U.N. and the other party that, in its view, the truce terms are not being observed and that the agreement must therefore be terminated.

On Jan. 13, 1948, a preliminary step towards a federated United States of Indonesia was taken by the setting up in Batavia of an interim Federal Government for Indonesia headed by Dr. van Mook as President and including representatives of the N.E.I. Government and of the various negaras and daerahs. In view of its existing political difficulties with the Netherlands, the Republic of Indonesia was not represented in this Government, it being, however, announced in Batavia that several seats had been reserved for the Republic when political difficulties had been resolved.

The members of the interim Federal Government, who included both Indonesians and Netherlanders and were designated Secretaries of State, were as follows:

Dr. Hubertus van Mook, President.

Raden Abdulkadir Widjojoatmodjo, Deputy President and Secretary for General Affairs.

Prof. Hossain Djajadiningrat, Foreign Affairs and Education.

Mr. H. van der Wal, Home Affairs.

Lt.-Col. Soeria Santoso, Internal Security.

Mr. T. Dzoelkarnain, Justice.

Mr. E. W. Alons, Finance.

Mr. J. E. van Hoogstraten, Economic Affairs.

Dr. J. E. Karamoy, Health.

Mr. B. Kryger, Social Affairs.

Mr. C. J. Warners, Transport, Power, and Mining.

Mr. A. M. Semawi, Waterways and Reconstruction.

Mr. Wisaksono Wirjodihardjo, Fisheries and Forestry.

Pangeran Kartanegara, Autonomous Administration.

Mr. B. S. van Deinse, Shipping.

Responsibility for the military and naval forces in the East Indies remained under the direction of the Dutch military and naval commanders-in-chief, General Spoor and Vice-Admiral Pinke.

Among the Indonesian members of the Interim Government, Raden Abdulkadir Widjojoatmodjo, a Javanese, was Deputy Lieutenant-Governor-General to Dr. van Mook, formerly served in the Dutch consular service, was Adviser to the N.E.I. Government in Australia during the war, and led the N.E.I. delegation in the Renville negotiations. Prof. Hossain Djajadiningrat, a leading Indonesian personality, was on the faculty of the High School of Law in Batavia, had served on the N.E.I. State Council (an advisory body to the Governor-General), and is not associated with any of the Indonesian political parties. Mr. Dzoelkarnain, a lawyer, represented East Sumatra, was associated with the claims of that territory to be an independent negara and played a prominent part in the Renville negotiations as a member of the N.E.I. delegation. Dr. Karamoy, a physician, and a graduate of Leiden and Düsseldorf universities, represented Menado (Celebes) in the Interim Government; Pangeran Kartamegara, member of a family of Borneo Sultans, represented the daerah of East Borneo; Lt.-Col. Santoso, a graduate of the Breda Military College in Holland, played a prominent part in the underground movement during the Japanese occupation; Mr. Semawi represented the negara of East Indonesia; and Mr. Wirjodihardjo is Burgomaster of Buitenzorg (Java).

In the Republic of Indonesia, the Cabinet headed by Mr. Amir Sjarifoeddin resigned on Jan. 23, 1948, after the signing of the Renville agreement, following strong attacks by extremist Indonesian nationalists who accused the Republican Government of having given way to Dutch demands in concluding the agreement. The Republican President, Dr. Soekarno, thereupon commissioned Dr. Mohamed Hatta (non-party), the Vice-President, to form a new administration. On Jan. 31, 1948, Dr. Hatta announced the members of the new Government, which included many members of the former administration and was drawn mainly from the Masjoemi (Moslem) Party and the Indonesian National Party (Partai Nasional Indonesia, or PNI.), the two leading political groups, but excluded all Socialist and Left-wing members:

Dr. Mohamed Hatta (non-party), Prime Minister and Defence.

Dr. H. A. Salim (Partai Serikat Islam Indonesia), Foreign Affairs.

Dr. Soekiman (Masjoemi), Home Affairs.

Mr. Maramis (P.N.I.), Finance.

Mr. Soesanto (P.N.I.), Justice.

Dr. Ali Sastroamidjojo (P.N.I.), Education.

Mr. S. Prawiranegara (Masjoemi), Social Welfare.

Mr. Djoeanda (non-party), Public Works.

Dr. Leimena (Christian Party), Health.

Mr. Koesnan (P.N.I.), Labour and Social Affairs.

Mr. Soepeno (non-party), Reconstruction

Mr. Kasima (Catholic Party), Food.

Mr. Kiai Mansoer (Masjoemi), Religious Affairs.

Dr. Mohamed Natsir (Masjoemi), Information.

The Sultan of Jogjakarta (non-party), Minister of State.

Among prominent members of the former Cabinet to retain office were Dr. Salim (whose party is a dissident fraction of the Masjoemi), Dr. Leimena, Dr. Sastroamidjojo, and the Sultan of Jogjakarta, whilst the most prominent of the retired Ministers were, in addition to Mr. Sjarifoeddin himself, Mr. A. K. Gani, Mr. Setiadjit Soegondo, and Dr. Mohamed Roem.

Dr. Hatta, on forming his new Cabinet, announced that it would carry out the Renville agreement, would continue negotiations with the Dutch through the U.N. Good Offices Committee, and would also carry out measures of national reconstruction in the Republic. Simultaneously with the announcement of the new Cabinet, Radio Jogjakarta stated that the Republican delegation which would continue the negotiations with the Dutch would be headed by Dr. Mohamed Roem in place of Mr. Sjarifoeddin, assisted by Dr. Sastroamidjojo, the Minister of Education, and other members (Dr. Roem, a member of the progressive wing of the Masjoemi, held office in both the Sjarifoeddin and Sjahrir Cabinets, in the former of which he was Minister for Home Affairs, and was a member of the Republican delegation which signed the Linggadjati Agreement).

Following the Renville agreement, the Committee of Good Offices recommenced discussions on March 15, 1948, alternately with the Dutch in Batavia and with the Indonesians in Jogjakarta.

The major issues dividing the Dutch and Indonesian delegations and preventing the conclusion of a political agreement were analysed by the Committe of Good Offices in a report to the Security Council on June 23, 1948.

The Committee, whilst noting that the truce continued to be observed by both sides, adduced the following reasons for the continuing deadlock in the negotiations: (a) the ways and means by which the United States of Indonesia should come into being; (b) the place of the Indonesian Republic in the Federation; (c) the allocation of powers between the Federation and the proposed Netherlands-Indonesian Union; (d) the failure to achieve an at least partial return to normal economic conditions following the Renville agreement; (e) resentment in the Indonesian Republic at the prior creation of an interim Federal Government, and at the creation of various negaras and daerahs by the Dutch authorities in different parts of Java, Sumatra, and Madura.

Reporting on the situation since the signing of the Renville agreement, the Committee stated in its report to the Security Council: "The Committee has gained the impression that the major issues dividing the parties are the very issues which always divided them, and which the Linggadjati Agreement has failed to resolve. It therefore wonders whether it has so far helped the parties to achieve anything concrete other than a military truce. The Netherlands and Indonesian authorities, bound by their cease-fire agreement, are eyeing one another across the status quo line with reserve and suspicion. Although important agreements for the resumption of normal trade and commerce between territories under the control of the Republic and those outside have been reached in principle, no significant increase in the volume of trade in and out of Republican-controlled areas can yet be reported. Such an increase will take place only if the agreements are implemented satisfactorily, but the Committee doubts whether full implementation is likely until a political settlement is reached. The difficulty of the political negotiations is show by the fact that both par-ties evidently consider the Renville agreement as not constituting an agreement in the full sense of the word, but simply as a basis for the discussion of a political settlement. The point whether the Renville principles were to take effect when the parties accepted them, or will become effective only when a political agreement has been reached, has never as yet been definitely settled and continues to be a fertile source of misunderstanding and dispute." After stating that "lack of progress towards the closing of the considerable gap between the positions of the two parties had "recently begun to have an unwholesome effect on the general atmosphere," the report added: "The chief long-term problem, in the Committee's view, remains the division of powers between the Netherlands-Indonesian Union and the Federation of Indonesia as a member of that Union. On this essential point the Netherlands delegation wants the assignment to the Union of func-tions -- particularly of a military and judicial nature -- which the Republic insists should belong to the members individually.

In the Security Council itself, the Dutch-Indonesian dispute was again brought up when the Indonesian delegate to the U.N., Mr. Palar, drew attention on June 10, 1948, to the recent emergence of the autonomous negaras of Madura and West Java, which, he alleged, were created under Dutch auspices, were subservient to the Netherlands Government, and were aimed at "cutting the ground" from under the feet of the Indonesian Republic, with which the Dutch were "ostensibly supposed to be negotiating." Dr. Van Kleffens, the Netherlands delegate, denied that Madura and West Java were "puppet" States as alleged by Mr. Palar; declared that the peoples of those States had shown, by free plebiscite, that they did not desire the "stringent unitarianism" of the Republic of Indonesia; claimed that the emergence of the negaras as sovereign independent States of the Indonesian Federation had taken place through the democratic processes based on the "Renville principles" criticized the "negative attitude" of the Indonesian Republic in the negotiations for a political settlement; and alleged that the leaders of the Republic had protested against the emergence of the negaras because they had "never given up their hopes of controlling all of the East Indies instead of being just one unit in the United States of Indonesia."

On July 23, 1948, the Indonesian Republic announced its intention of breaking off the discussions with the Netherlands.

The official announcement from Jogjakarta said that this decision had been taken because, since the Dutch rejection 5 weeks' earlier of the proposals put forward by the U.S. and Australian members of the Committee, no further proposals had been forthcoming from the Dutch side to put an end to the deadlock; that, during this period, the Netherlands delegation had given no reason for their rejection of the proposals mentioned; and that in consequence, the Republic felt that further political discussions were useless. The Republican Minister of Information, Dr. Natsir, in a statement the same day, said that the decision would not affect the truce agreement, nor discussions on economic and financial matters, and that the Republic was ready to resume the political negotiations as soon as a "new reasonable basis" for such discussions was forthcoming.

The Good Offices Committee, in a report to the Security Council on Dec. 3, 1948, again drew attention the growing seriousness of the Indonesian situation resulting from the failure to reach a political agreement, and described the talks between the Ministerial Mission and the Republican Government (at the time in progress) as a "serious and possibly final attempt" of the parties to reach a settlement.

After stating that, despite all its efforts, the Committee had made no progress whatsoever in finding a settlement of the 3-year-old dispute between Holland and the Indonesian Republic, the report commented that "the Netherlands delegation has been reluctant to consider proposals put forward by the Australian and U.S. representatives on the Committee, and neither party has come forward with proposals for an overall settlement of the dispute." This delay in achieving a settlement, it was emphasized, entailed serious economic and political consequences of a fourfold character, viz., (1) there had been a "serious and rapid" deterioration in the

normal trade of the Republic,which had come to a virtual standstill and
which, if the present conditions continued, threatened to result in economic
chaos and in the delaying of the economic rehabilitation of Indonesia as a
whole; (2) the delay had imposed a strain on the Republican Government,
which had had to face internal difficulties, and which was showing increasing opposition to the action of the Dutch authorities in negotiating with the
non-Republican parts of Indonesia, which, it was feared, might lead to the
establishment of an interim Federal Government for Indonesia without Republican participation; (3) political tension between the Dutch and the Republic had increased as a result of the prolonged deadlock; and (4) the 10-
month-old truce agreement was, as a consequence, in danger of breaking
down.

The Committee pointed out that during the period covered by the report (June-November 1948) the situation in Indonesia had become "critically
unstable" and made a solution imperative; that during this period no political negotiations had taken place under the Committee's auspices, nor any
proposals put forward by either party; that both parties had made numerous allegations of local infringements of the truce; and that the Committee's
military observers had reported that these infractions (which had occurred
both in Java and Sumatra) arose from an "unfortunate readiness on both
sides to resort to direct action with firearms."

On Dec. 16, 1948, it was announced from The Hague that the Netherlands Government had rejected proposals contained in a letter from Dr.
Hatta (whose contents were not made public) suggesting further negotiations
after the breakdown of the discussions with the Ministerial Mission. The
announcement said that Dr. Hatta's letter was of an "informal" character
and sent on his own initiative; that past experience had "demonstrated that
Dr. Hatta could not always speak for the Republic"; and that negotiations
could be resumed only if the Republic ended truce violations and if, by an
"immediate binding declaration," it would agree to the conditions as previously laid down by the Netherlands Government.

The Dutch communiqué of Dec. 18 announcing the breaking off of the
truce agreement was worded as follows:

"Time and again it has proved impossible to enlist the co-operation
of the Republic for an effective implementation of the agreements that have
been concluded. Arrangements for implementation of the Linggadjati Agreement, though accepted by the Republican Prime Minister, were repudiated
by the Republican Government in Jogjakarta. The same happened shortly
afterwards with the arrangement concluded with Mr. Sjarifoeddin. Recently the expectations roused by the discussions between Dr. Stikker and Dr.
Hatta were nullified after the opposition in Jogjakarta raised its voice.
Subsequently, a letter was received from Dr. Hatta in which he endeavour-
ed to clarify misunderstandings which in his opinion had arisen, and in
which he gave his further views regarding a number of points. No mention
was made of any action to combat infringements of the truce, whilst it was
pointed out that the letter had a personal, unofficial and confidential charac-

ter. Moreover, reservations were made concerning a number of essential points which raised questions as to the exact meaning of this communication. Since this letter alone could not constitute a point of departure for further discussions, the Netherlands Government decided to enable the Republican Government to supplement it by a binding declaration regarding a number of points, in particular (1) the incorporation of the Republic in the Federal organization on the same footing as the other Federal areas; (2) the regulations of the position of the High Commissioner of the Crown in the transition period; (3) the provisions regarding the Federal forces, the state of war and siege, and the state of security; (4) the taking forthwith of measures necessary for effectively terminating infringements of the trace and evacuating infiltrants. If such a declaration had been obtained, the Government would have been prepared to reopen discussions.

A reply from the Republic has not been received within the fixed period; neither has a prolongation of the truce been requested ... In these circumstances every possibility that an amelioration of the untenable situation in Indonesia would be obtainable at short notice was therefore lacking. In particular, it should be pointed out in this respect that the number of violations of the truce is increasing daily. Military commanders in Republican territory have organized infiltrations of thousands of Republican soldiers into non-Republican areas, where assaults are being committed continuously, in particular against Indonesian officials. Since August this year hundreds of these Indonesians have been murdered, while many more were wounded or kidnapped. It also became apparent that the Republic, in view of the proposed establishment of a Federal Interim Government by Jan. 1, 1949, had prepared large-scale armed action in all non-Republican territories, while people who were willing to co-operate with the Netherlands were being constantly threatened and intimidated.

In these circumstances the Netherlands Government considers it impossible to enter again into discussions which, as experience has shown, do not offer new prospects. Since the Republican Government is taking no effective measures to combat infringements of the truce, the Netherlands Government cannot consider itself committed to maintain the truce agreements, or to tolerate any longer the fact that armed activities in other areas are being directed from Republican territory. These reasons have finally compelled the Netherlands Government to avail itself of the provisions of Art. 10 of the truce agreement and to announce its decision to terminate this agreement and resume its freedom of action.

The Netherlands Government is convinced that both in the Republican Government and among the population in Republican territory there are many who are only too eager to co-operate in constructing the Federation to which the Netherlands will transfer sovereignty as soon as possible. "The action which has been ordered is not directed against them. It is directed against the terrorists and undisciplined elements in the Republic who render all constructive efforts impossible. The future constitutional incorporation of the Republican territory will take place on the basis of the

principles of the Linggadjati and <u>Renville</u> agreements and the consultations
now prescribed by the Netherlands Constitution. A decree concerning the
Government of Indonesia during the transition period had been promulgated
to-day which explicitly leaves open the possibility of such incorporation on
the basis of further consultation with representatives of the territories concerned. The Netherlands Governments will fully honour its pledges regarding constitutional reforms and the creation of an independent sovereign
United States of Indonesia, linked as an equal partner with the Netherlands
in a Netherlands-Indonesian Union. The Netherlands have demonstrated
their preparedness to contribute to the opening of the road to freedom in
Indonesia. This freedom, however, can only be achieved if there are ample
safeguards against domination by extremist elements in the Republic who
render a democratic order impossible."

Following the breaking off of the truce agreement by the Netherlands
Government, strong forces of Dutch ground troops, paratroops, and Marines crossed the "van Mook line" at a number of points into Republican
territory in Java and Sumatra and effected landings from the sea on both
islands, meeting with little resistance and rapidly securing control of all
Republican territories. Jogjakarta, the Republican capital, fell within a
few hours of the opening of operations, its airfield being captured intact by
Dutch paratroops forming the spearhead of the attack. Surakarta, in Central Java (second city of the Republic, with a population of about 500,000),
and the port of Rembang, were taken on Dec. 21; Bukittinggi, capital of the
Republican territory in Sumatra, was occupied without opposition on Dec.
22; Serang, capital of Bantam Province (Western Java), fell on Dec. 24; and
Madioen was taken on Dec. 26, the Netherlands communiqué of the latter
date stating that with the capture of Madioen all major cities and highways
throughout the whole of Java were in Dutch hands. On Dec. 27 it was announced in Batavia that the Dutch Army had occupied all key-points in the
Republic, and that Republican losses had been "relatively light" owing to
the fact that there had been "practically no resistance" by the Indonesians.
The whole of Java was reported under Dutch military control on Dec. 31,
and on Jan. 2, 1949, General Spoor announced that all military action there
had ended apart from small-scale mopping-up operations; the number of
Dutch casualties since the commencement of operations on Dec. 19 was
given at 66 killed and 172 wounded, it being added that many Indonesian officers had voluntarily surrendered. The cessation of hostilities in Sumatra
(where the important Djambi oilfields had been captured intact on Dec. 30)
was likewise announced by General Spoor on Jan. 5, 1949.

During the operations, President Soekarno, Dr. Hatta, Dr. Salim,
General Soedirman, and other Republican leaders were taken prisoner at
Jogjakarta on Dec. 19 and placed under arrest, whilst Dr. Roem was cap-
tured and interned at Kalioerang on Dec. 22.

A report by General Spoor on Jan 1, 1949, said that all the Sumatran
oilfields had been preserved from destruction during the operations, but
that in Central Java the Republican "scorched earth" and demolition tactics

had in certain areas wrought considerable damage. In a survey of economic conditions issued on Jan. 4 by the Economic Dept. in Batavia, it was stated that the overall position in Java with regard to the rice supply was "not too bad," that prospects for the next food harvest were "good," and that important tobacco plantations, sugar refineries, and public utilities had escaped damage during the operations. The situation in Surakarta, however, was described as serious in view of large-scale demolitions by the Republicans before the Dutch forces entered the city, the damage including the blowing up of the railway station. the electric power-station, the water-works, and the telephone exchange, as well as other large buildings, whilst plantations in the Surakarta area were also badly damaged. The town of Magelang, in Central Java, was also said to have been severely damaged and "full of smoking ruins" when the Dutch forces entered, and oil installations at Tjepoe likewise to have been heavily damaged.

The Good Offices Committee, in a report to the Security Council on Dec. 20, said that the Netherlands Government had not given the proper notice, as laid down in the Renville agreement, of its intention to end the truce; that Mr. Merle Cochran, the U.S. chairman of the Committee, was informed of the Dutch intention only half-an-hour before hostilities actually commenced; that it was impossible to inform the other members of the Committee, who were then at Kalioerang; and that thus neither the Good Offices Committee as a whole, nor, as far as was known, the Republican Government, had been informed of the Dutch repudiation of the agreement, the Republican delegation in Batavia having only been informed 15 minutes before communications with Jogjakarta were suspended.

At the request of the U.S. and Australian Governments, and of the Good Offices Committee, the U.N. Security Council met in Paris on Dec. 22, 1948, to consider the situation in Indonesia which had arisen from the Dutch repudiation of the truce agreement and the resultant military action.

On Dec. 24, after lengthy debate, the Security Council adopted by 7 votes (U.S.A., Great Britain, China, Canada, Argentina, Colombia, Syria) to nil, with 4 abstentions (U.S.S.R., France, Belgium, Ukraine) a resolution embodying the original U.S.-Colombian-Syrian resolution and the Australian amendment, which in its final form (a) called on both parties to cease hostilities forthwith, (b) called for the immediate release of President Soekarno and other Indonesian leaders, and (c) instructed the Good Offices Committee to report to the Council on events in Indonesia since Dec. 19, 1948, and to observe and report on the compliance of the parties with (a) and (b).

Following the impasse caused by the Dutch "police action" against the Indonesian Republic in December 1948, and the subsequent internment of the Republican leaders in the island of Banka (see 9733 A), the U.N. Security Council met at Lake Success from Jan. 21-28, 1949, to consider the Indonesian situation, and on the latter date adopted a resolution, presented jointly by the U.S.A., China, Cuba, and Norway, calling on the Netherlands Government to create an interim Federal Government in Indonesia by March 15, 1949, and to transfer sovereignty to the United States of Indonesia as early as possible thereafter, and in any case not later than July 1, 1950. The detailed provisions of this resolution were as follows:

(1) The Netherlands Government was called on to discontinue military operations immediately; the Indonesian Republic was called on simultaneously to order its armed forces to cease guerrilla warfare; and both parties were urged to co-operate in the restoration of peace and the maintenance of law and order in the affected areas.

(2) The Netherlands Government was called on to release "immediately and unconditionally" all political prisoners arrested by them since Dec. 17, 1948 (the commencement of the "police action"); to facilitate the immediate return of the Republican leaders and officials to Jogjakarta (the capital of the Indonesian Republic); and to allow them to exercise their functions, including the administration of the Jogjakarta area, in full freedom.

(3) A "federal, independent, and sovereign" United States of Indonesia should be established at the earliest possible date on the basis of the principles set out in the Linggadjati and Renville agreements, and negotiations to this end should be undertaken as soon as possible between the Netherlands and the Indonesian Republic, with the assistance of the U.N. representatives in Indonesia. Specifically, it was laid down that (a) the establishment of an interim Federal Government, which should have powers of internal government in Indonesia prior to the formal transfer of sovereignty, should be effected not later than March 15, 1949; (b) elections should be held for an Indonesian Constituent Assembly not later than Oct. 1, 1949; (c) the Netherlands should transfer sovereignty to the U.S.I. "at the earliest possible date, and in any case not later than July 1, 1950."

(4) The U.N. Committee of Good Offices in Batavia would be renamed the U.N. Commission for Indonesia, would continue to act as representative of the Security Council, and would present to the Council the views of both sides in the Indonesian question. Specifically, the U.N. Commission would assist both parties in implementing the Security Council's resolution; would have authority to consult with representatives of areas in Indonesia other than those of the Republic; would observe any elections on behalf of the U.N.; would assist in achieving the earliest possible restoration of civil administration to the Indonesian Republic; and would make periodic reports to the Security Council.

c. Heavy criticism in the United Nations and continuing guerrilla resistance of the army of the Republic of Indonesia forced the Netherlands in 1949 to withdraw its troops and to transfer sovereignty to Indonesia as a partner in a Dutch-Indonesian Union. The following charter was signed on November 2, 1949 in The Hague.

Charter on the Transfer of Sovereignty.

This consisted of the following two Articles:

Art. 1. "The Kingdom of the Netherlands unconditionally and irrevocably transfers complete sovereignty over Indonesia to the Republic of the United States of Indonesia, as an independent and sovereign State ... The transfer of sovereignty shall take place at latest on Dec. 30, 1949."

Art. 2. This laid down that "in view of the fact that it has not been possible to reconcile the views of the two parties over New Guinea," the status quo of that territory would be maintained, "with the stipulation that within a year from the date of transfer of sovereignty to the U.S.I. the question of the political status of New Guinea be determined through negotiations between the U.S.I. and the Netherlands."

Statute of the Netherlands-Indonesian Union.

This consisted of a Preamble, 28 Articles, and an Annex on Human Rights, as follows:

Preamble. "The Kingdom of the Netherlands and the Republic of the United States of Indonesia, having decided on a basis of voluntariness, equality, and complete independence to call into being a friendly co-operation with each other, and, in order to effectuate the future co-operation, to create the Netherlands-Indonesian Union,

have agreed to lay down in this Statute of the Union the basis of their mutual relationship as independent and sovereign States,

thereby considering that nothing in this Statute shall be interpreted as excluding any form of co-operation not mentioned therein, or co-operation in any field not mentioned therein, the need of which may be felt in the future by both partners."

Character of the Union.

Art. 1. The Union "effectuates the organized co-operation between the Kingdom of the Netherlands and the Republic of the U.S.I., on the basis of voluntariness and equal status with equal rights," and does not prejudice the status of either of the two partners as an independent sovereign State.

Purpose of the Union.

Art. 2. The Union "aims at co-operation of the partners for the promotion of their common interests. This co-operation shall take place with respect to matters lying primarily in the fields of foreign relations and defence, and as far as necessary finance, and also as regards matters of an economic and cultural nature."

Art. 3. Both partners undertake to base their form of government on the principles of democracy, and recognize the fundamental human rights and freedoms listed in the Annex.

Functioning of the Union.

Art. 4. "All decisions in the Union shall be taken in agreement between the two partners."

The Head of the Union.

Art. 5. The Head of the Union is H.M. Queen Juliana of the Netherlands, and her lawful successors to the Crown of the Netherlands.

Art. 6. The Head of the Union "embodies the concept of voluntary and lasting co-operation between the partners."

The Organs of the Union.

Art. 7. Union conferences shall be held twice yearly, or as often as the partner deem necessary. Unless otherwise agreed, the Netherlands and Indonesia will each be represented at such conferences by three Ministers, who will have equal responsibilities.

Art. 8. "Ministers participating in such conferences will remain responsible to the respective organs of the partners on the basis of their respective Constitutions."

Art. 9. Ministerial Conferences may, as circumstances require, appoint committees on which each partner will be equally represented.

Art. 10. Regular co-operation and contact shall be achieved between the Netherlands and Indonesian Parliaments. The first inter-Parliamentary discussions will take place within eight months after the establishment of the Provisional Parliament of the U.S.I.

Art. 11. The Union will possess a permanent Secretariat. Each of the partners will appoint a Secretary-General by yearly rotation.

Decisions and Joint Regulations.

Art. 12. Decisions taken at Ministerial Conferences of the Union must be approved by both parties, and those concerning the enactment of joint regulations require ratification by both the Netherlands and Indonesian Parliaments.

Union Court of Arbitration.

Art. 13. A Union Court of Justice will be established to adjudicate on all matters concerning legal disputes arising out of the Statute of the Union, or out of any agreements or joint regulations entered into between the Netherlands and Indonesia. Such disputes may be presented to the Court by either party, or by both parties jointly.

Art. 14. The Union Court will consist of three Netherlands and three Indonesian members, serving for a 10-year period. Members must retire on reaching the age of 65. A Netherlander and an Indonesian will in turn act as chairman of the Court by yearly rotation.

Art. 15. The Union Court will take its decisions by majority vote. In case of a tie vote, the International Court of Justice, or other international authority, shall be requested to designate a person of another nationality to sit on the Union Court as an extraordinary member and to take part in the consideration of, and decision on, the dispute.

Art. 16. The Court's rules of procedure and organization, and the regulation of its activities, will be laid down in a special regulation.

Art. 17. Both the Netherlands and Indonesia undertake to comply with the decisions of the Union Court, and to implement those decisions in their territories.

Art. 18. "In case of conflict between provisions of the law of the partners and of public corporations within their jurisdiction on the one side, and the Union Statute or any agreement between the partners or a joint regulation on the other, the latter category of provisions shall prevail."

Art. 19. Both the Netherlands and Indonesia reserve their rights under international law to solicit the decision of an international judge or arbitrator in cases where both partners consider that the Union Court lacks competence, or in cases where the Court declares itself incompetent in any particular matter.

Mutual Co-operation.

Arts. 20-23. These Articles state that the principles governing co-operation between the Netherlands and the U.S.I. in the fields of foreign relations, defence, financial and economic matters, and cultural relations, are set forth in special agreements attached to the Statute of the Union (see below).

Citizenship.

Art. 24. Without prejudice to any special arrangements made, or still to be made, between the Netherlands and the U.S.I., both partners agree that the nationality of citizens of one partner shall not constitute an objection to holding offices within the jurisdiction of the other partner except (a) in the case of offices the holder of which is responsible to a representative assembly, unless the law should provide otherwise; (b) "those political, authoritative, judicial, and leading offices which are specified as such by law." Furthermore, neither party shall discriminate against the special interests of citizens and corporate bodies of the other party within its jurisdiction; such citizens and corporate bodies will in no case receive less favourable treatment than that accorded to citizens and corporate bodies of a third State.

Exchange of High Commissioners.

Art. 25. Each partner shall accredit a High Commissioner to the other, possessing diplomatic status with Ambassadorial rank.

Special Provisions.

Art. 26. Unless otherwise agreed, each partner shall bear one-half of the expenses of the Union, further provisions in regard to such expenses being established by common agreement.

Art. 27. All official documents issued by the Conference of Ministers or other Union organs shall be in the Netherlands and Indonesian languages, both texts having equal authenticity.

Art. 28. The Statute of the Union, and the agreements attached thereto, may be registered with the United Nations in accordance with Art. 102 of the U.N. Charter.

Annex on Human Rights.

This recapitulates the fundamental rights and freedoms which both the Netherlands and the U.S.I. pledge themselves to uphold "without discrimination of any kind on the grounds of race, colour, sex, language, religion, national or social origin, property, or birth." It lays down inter alia that all persons are entitled by law to equal treatment and protection; that no-one may be arrested or detained except by due process of law; and that both partners recognize the rights of inviolability of domicile, freedom and secrecy of correspondence, freedom of thought, conscience and religion, freedom of opinion and expression, freedom of peaceful association and assembly, freedom to hold property, freedom from arbitrary deprivation of property, freedom of employment and of just conditions of work, freedom to join and form trade unions, and freedom to education and to social security.

The principal points of the agreement on transitional measures, and of the other agreements referred to in Arts. 20-23 of the Union Statute, are summarized below.

Transitional Measures. The division of the U.S.I. into component States shall be established finally by the Constituent Assembly of the U.S.I. in conformity with the provisions of the Provisional Constitution, on the understanding that a plebiscite will be held, on the recommendation and under the supervision of the U.N. Indonesian Commission, in any territory on the question of whether that territory should form a component State of the U.S.I. Each component State will be given the opportunity to ratify the final Constitution.

All powers formerly exercised by the Governor-General of the Netherlands East Indies shall, by virtue of the transfer of power, pass to the U.S.I. and its component States. The Rulers of the component States are, as from the transfer of power, ipso facto liberated from their oath of allegiance to H.M. the Queen of the Netherlands.

The Kingdom of the Netherlands undertakes to promote the membership of the United States of Indonesia in the United Nations.

Military Agreement. Each partner will bear full responsibility for the defence of its own territory, but may, if requested by the other partner, lend to the latter such aid as may be desired. This aid will consist of the training of officers, N.C.O.s, specialized military personnel, and civil auxiliary personnel, in making available such personnel or materials as may be requested, and in the provision of facilities for maintenance and repairs. Should one of the partners request the other to make available units of the fighting forces in the other's jurisdiction, a special agreement can be concluded to this effect. Both partner shall exchange Military Missions, and will consult with each other in the case of imminent attack on either or both of them. The subjects of one of the partners may not be compelled to serve in the fighting forces of the other.

Netherlands land forces will be withdrawn from Indonesia within six months of the transfer of power, and the Royal Netherlands Navy will be withdrawn from Indonesian waters with a year. The Netherlands will, however, on request, provide aid in Indonesian maritime defence insofar as

Indonesia is not able to fulfil this task herself. A Netherlands naval officer will be appointed commander of the Surabaya naval base, with responsibility to the Indonesian Minister of Defence.

Economic and Financial Agreement. Rights, concessions and properties granted under the law of the Netherlands East Indies, and valid on the date of the transfer of power, will be recognized by the U.S.I., which undertakes, insofar as this has not already been done, to restore such rights, concessions, etc., to their lawful owners. The U.S.I. will, however, reserve the right to "make an investigation in respect of important rights, concessions, and licences granted after March 1, 1942, which may influence the economic policy of the U.S.I." Any "expropriation, nationalization, liquidation, compulsory cession, or transfer of properties and rights" undertaken after such investigation "shall take place for the public benefit only, in accordance with legally prescribed procedure, and -- in the absence of agreement between the parties -- against guaranteed indemnification, to be fixed by judicial decision at the real value of the object involved."

Existing and new enterprises, estates, etc., will have the possibility of renewal of rights, concessions, and licences required for their operation. Such enterprises will give facilities for the participation of Indonesian capital when this is justified from a business point of view. Netherlands nationals and corporate bodies will enjoy treatment in Indonesia not less favourable than that accorded to third countries, and "foreigners of all nations will have equal rights in the participation of trade with Indonesia and in the economic activity and industrial development of the country."

Apart from the general obligation on all employers that their enterprises shall be conducted in accordance with the laws of Indonesia, such employers shall, "in the interests of social peace and order and for the improvement of social conditions," co-operate inter alia in (a) the institution of organized consultation between managements and workers; (b) the promotion of higher living standards for the workers; (c) improvements in housing and other spheres of social welfare; (d) the inclusion, within the earliest possible period, of eligible Indonesians in the direction, management, and staffs of enterprises.

In the financial field it was agreed that the Netherlands and Indonesia should each aim at "a sound monetary system based on the principles expressed in the Bretton Woods agreements," and that the monetary policy of the Union "shall aim at achieving and maintaining a stable internal and external value of the currency, and at promoting free convertibility of exchange." The U.S.I., with Netherlands support, will seek early admission to the International Monetary Fund.

The debt agreement reached between the two partners provided that the U.S.I. would resume responsibility for (a) a number of consolidated loans, (b) debts to third countries calculated as of Dec. 31, 1949, (c) debts to the Kingdom of the Netherlands calculated as of the same date, and (d) all internal debts at the time of the transfer of sovereignty. Under (b),

Indonesia will assume responsibility for the U.S. Export-Import Bank loan
to Indonesia (Oct. 29, 1948) within the framework of the E.C.A.
($15,000,000 outstanding on Dec. 31, 1949); a U.S. "line of credit" granted
to the N.E.I. Government on May 28, 1947, for the purchase of U.S. sur-
plus property ($62,550,000 outstanding on Dec. 31, 1949); a loan from Can-
ada on Oct. 9, 1945 (Can. $15,452,000 outstanding on Dec. 31, 1949); and
a settlement between Australia and the Government of Indonesia of Aug. 17,
1949 (£A.8,500,000 outstanding on Dec. 31, 1949). For all the above-men-
tioned debts the U.S.I. assumes responsibility for payment of both interest
and amortization.

The total amount of the debts taken over by Indonesia was 4,300,000,000
guilders -- viz., 3,000,000,000 guilders internal debt and 1,300,000,000
guilders external debt. This compared with an amount of 6,100,000,000
guilders originally submitted by the Netherlands as outstanding in August
1949, and of 2,000,000,000 guilders (the total debt in March 1942) which
the Indonesians had proposed to take over before a compromise was eventually reached.

Agreement on Citizenship. Netherlanders in Indonesia above the age
of 18 retain Netherlands nationality, but, if born in Indonesia, or resident
there for at least six months, may opt for Indonesian nationality. Netherlands subjects who before the transfer of power belonged to the indigenous
population of Indonesia acquire Indonesian nationality as from the transfer
of power. If persons in the latter category were born outside Indonesia,
and reside in the Kingdom of the Netherlands (including Metropolitan Holland, Surinam, and the Netherlands Antilles) or in foreign countries, they
may, if they desire, opt for Netherlands nationality within six months.
Persons under the age of 18 will possess the nationality of their father or
mother and married women will possess the status of their husbands.

Agreement on Foreign Relations. Both partners shall co-operate in
the field of foreign relations, and, if they so decide, may, through the Conference of Ministers, make provision for joint of common representation
in international intercourse. Without derogation of the principle that each
partner shall conduct its own foreign relations and determine its own foreign
policy, they shall together aim at co-ordinating their foreign policy as
much as possible, and will consult with each other thereon. Neither partner shall conclude a treaty, or perform any other juridical act in the international field, without prior consultation with the other. Should one of the
partners not have an accredited diplomatic representative in a foreign country, its interests in that country will be represented by the other partner.

Agreement on Cultural Co-operation. Cultural relations between the
Netherlands and Indonesia will have "a universal character and will aim at
the realization of the expansion of the free human mind." To foster such
co-operation, a joint committee of 14 members (seven from each side) will
be appointed by the two Governments, whose recommendations will be presented to the Conference of Ministers. Specifically, the Netherlands and
Indonesia undertake (a) "the promotion in their own country of a reasonable

knowledge of the fundamental elements of the other partner's culture"; (b) the diffusion of such knowledge through the media of books, films, radio broadcasts, the Press, exhibitions, etc.; (c) the exchange of professors, teachers, and students in the fields of science, the arts, and education; (d) the establishment of cultural institutions in the territory of the other partner; (e) the provision of opportunities for mutual scientific research; (f) the free admission of books, newspapers, and periodicals of the other partner. It was also stated that both partners would co-operate "in making an inventory of the state of science in Indonesia at the moment of the transfer of sovereignty, in particular with respect to natural sciences, techniques, and medical science."

Agreement on Civil Servants. The U.S.I. agreed, as from the transfer of sovereignty, to take into its employment all Civil Government officials of Netherlands nationality then working in Indonesia, and for two years thereafter to make no "unfavourable alterations" in their legal position. Thereafter, the U.S.I. may at its discretion grant any officials "honourable discharge' under specified terms of compensation relating to the various categories of officials.

DOCUMENT XVI

d. The formal transfer of sovereignty took place on December 27, 1949 at the Royal Palace in Amsterdam. At that occasion Queen Juliana gave the following speech:

The assumption of sovereignty by the Republic of the United States of Indonesia, its relinquishment by the Kingdom of the Netherlands, and the conclusion of a Union, is one of the most deeply moving events of the times. It is on the one hand moving because of the unnaturalness of the course it has taken, and on the other because never before has it emerged more clearly how deep is the sympathy borne by the two nations towards each other. No longer do we stand partially opposed to one another. We have now taken our stations side by side, however, much we may be bruised and torn, carrying the scars of rancour and regret.

These documents represent a result attained in both countries by democratic means. Both countries feel sufficiently strong and resilient to start afresh, East and West working to one end....Our confidence for the times to come rests on the good and true elements, of whatever conviction, of the two countries, as these have always in this world proved to be the pioneers of better times, though sometimes temporarily misunderstood and sometimes even failing to find each other.

Immeasurable is the satisfaction of a nation that finds its liberty realized, however immense the burden shouldered by the young nation. In the Netherlands this is viewed with solicitude. But at this moment and in this place I would state emphatically that in the Netherlands one and all concur with the principle of transfer of sovereignty. I appeal to all to co-operate loyally in the new system. The Netherlands are in readiness to render assistance as soon as and when Indonesia asks for it. Willingness to stand by her arises from a deeply rooted attachment.

It is a privilege to perform this Act of Transfer as it stands in history, or rather, in the face of God, who knows why this going together in freedom was not achieved sooner, nor later, and who knows the failing of generations, but who also sees whether we can serve in the plan for the progress of mankind. May this now be so.

SOURCES OF DOCUMENTS

I   A. Barnouw, Coming After (1948, Rutgers University Press).

II John William Burgon, The Life and Times of Sir Thomas Gresham, Vol. II (1839).

III L. P. Gachard, La Correspondance de Guillaume le Taciturne, Vol. III.

IV Lord Somers, Tracts, reprinted as Old South Leaflet No. 72.

V   J. H. van Linschoten, Itinerario (Seventeenth century translation, re-edited by Hakluyt Society in 1885).

VI G. van de Veer, The Three Voyages of Willem Barentsz (Seventeenth century translation re-edited by Hakluyt Society in 1876).

VII P. de la Cour, The Interest of Holland (translation of 1702).

VIII J. van der Capellen tot den Pol, Aan het Volk van Nederland.

IX H. T. Colenbrander, Gedenkstukken der Algemene Geschiedenis van Nederland, Vol. VII (The Hague, 1907).

X   H. T. Colenbrander, Inlijving en Opstand (1913).

XI Bijdragen en Mededelingen van het Historisch Genootschap, Vol. 71 (Groningen, 1957).

XII Princess Wilhelmina, Lonely But Not Alone (McGraw-Hill, 1958).

XIII Underground newspaper quoted in Het Woord als Wapen (1952).

XIV H. T. Colenbrander, Inlijving en Opstand (1913).

XV S. D. van Campen, The Quest for Security (The Hague, 1958).

XVIa H. J. van Mook, Indonesie, Nederland en de Wereld (Amsterdam, 1949).

XVIb Keesing's Contemporary Archives, January 15-22, 1949.

XVIc Keesing's Contemporary Archives, January 15-22, 1949; March 11-18, 1950.

XVId Keesing's Contemporary Archives, March 11-18, 1950.

Aalberse, Minister, 51
Adabold, Bishop of Utrecht, 2
Albert of Austria, 17, 18
Albrecht of Saxony, 8
Alva, Duke of, 11, 12
Amsberg, Claus von, 63
Anne, daughter of King George
  III of England, 33, 34
Antoon, Duke of Brabant, 4
Arminius, 18
Augereau, General, 38

Barentsz, 16
Beatrix, Crown Princess, 54, 63
Beerenbrouck, Ruys de, 48
Bergen, 10
Bergh, Van den, 21
Bernard of Galen, Bishop of
  Munster, 26, 27
Bernard of Lippe-Biesfeld,
  Prince, 54, 57
Bismarck, First Chancellor of
  German Empire, 46
Blake, 24
Blaskowitz, General, 57
Borgesius, Goeman, 49
Borselen, Frank van, 5
Bosch, General, van den, 42
Bosch, Hieronymus, 8
Boudewijn, Count of Flanders, 2
Breughel, the Elder, Pieter, 8
Brunswick, Field Marshal, 34
Buat, Captain, 25

Caesar, Julius, 1
Carlos-Hugo of Bourbon-Parma,
  Prince, 63
Casimir, Ernst, of Nassau, 20,
  21
Casimir, John, 14
Catherine of Russia, 35
Charlemagne, 1, 2
Charles of Austria, 31, 32
Charles of Egmond, 8, 10, 11, 12
Charles, Duke of Guelders, 9
Charles the Bold, Duke of
  Burgundy, 6, 7
Charles I of England, 22, 23

Charles II of England, 26, 27, 28,
  28, 29, 30, 31
Charles VII of France, 6
Charles V, German Emperor,
  King of Spain, Lord of the
  Netherlands, 8, 9, 10, 13
Charles X of Sweden, 25
Civilis, Julius, 1
Clive, Lord, 34
Cock, De, of Ulrum, 43
Coen, Jan P., 19, 20
Colbert, 25
Coppello, Kappeyne van de, 47
Coppenhole, Jan van, 8
Coutereel, Pieter, 4
Crijnssen, Abraham, 26

Daendels, 37
Deterding, Sir H., 54
Deventer, 15
Diederich of Alsace, Count of
  Flanders, 2
Doorman, Admiral, 56
Drees, 57, 58, 61
Duyn, van de, 39

Edward III, King of England, 4
Edward VI, King of England, 6
Elizabeth of Gorlitz, 4, 6
Elizabeth, Queen of England,
  15
Emanuel II, Maximilian, of
  Bavaria, 31
Emma, Queen, 48
Engelbrechtsz, Cornelis, 8
Erasmus, Desiderius, 6
Ernest, Peter, Count of
  Mansfield, 16
Essen, Jan van, 9

Falck, 39
Farnese, Alexander, Duke of
  Parma, 14, 15, 16
Ferdinand of Aragon, 8
Ferdinand of Brunswick, 36
Ferdinand, Joseph, 31
Floris, Frans, 8
Floris V, Count of Holland, 3
Foulkes, General, 57

Francis I, King of France, 9
Frederick, Emperor of Germany, 7
Frederick, Prince of Orange, 41, 42
Frederick, William, 23
Fynje, Wybo, 37

Gaulle, Charles de, 62
Geelkerken, van C., 53
Geer, Premier de, 54
Gent, Bishop of, 40
Gerard, Balthasar, 14
Gerhardt, H., 47
Geyl, 53
Gomarus, 18
Granvelle, Cardinal de, 10, 11
Groningen, 9
Groot, Hugo de, 20
Guy of Dampierre, Count of Flanders, 3
Gwyde, Bishop of Utrecht, 3

Hall, Van, 45
Hamburg, Archbishop of, 2
Hatta, 57
Heemskerck, 16
Heemskert, Maarten van, 8
Hendrik, Duke of Mecklenburg-Schwerin, 49
Henriette d'Oultremont, 44
Henry of Bourbon, 16
Henry, Frederick, 20, 21, 22
Henry de Guise, 15
Henry V, King of England, 5
Henry III of France, 15, 16
Henry IV of France, 17
Heutsz, Van, 49
Heyn, Piet, 21
Hoffman, Melchior, 9
Hogendorp, Van, 39
Hogerbeets, 20
Holmes, Captain, 25
Hoogstraten, 10
Hoop, Van der, 52
Hoorne, 10, 12
Houten, S. van, 48
Hudson, Henry, 18

Humphrey, Duke of Gloucester, 5

Irene, Princess, 54, 63
Isabella of Castile, 8
Isabella, daughter of Philip II, 16, 17

Jacoba of Bavaria, 5
Jacobs, Aletta, 46
James II, 30
Jansz, Willem, 17
Johanna of Brabant, 4
Johanna, daughter of Ferdinand of Aragon, 8
John, Duke of Bavaria, 5
John II, Duke of Brabant, 3
John IV, Duke of Brabant, 5
John of Touraine, 5
Jones, John Paul, 35
Joseph I, Emperor of Austria, 32
Juan, Don, of Austria, 13, 14
Juliana, Queen, 50, 54, 59, 63, 64

Keyzer, Pieter, 17
Kruger, President of the Orange Free State, 49
Kuyper, Abraham, 47, 48, 49, 50

Lebrun, Charles-Francois, 38
Leicester, 15
Lemaire, Jacques, 19
Leopold, Emperor of Austria, 31
Leopold, Emperor of Germany, 28
Leopold, King of Belgium, 54
Leopold of Saxe-Coburg, King of Belgium, 42
Leyden, Lucas van, 8
Limburg, General van, 51
Linschoten, Jan Huyghen van, 16
Louis XI of France, 6, 7
Louis XIV of France, 25, 27, 30, 31
Luxemburg, 28
Luzac, 44

Maasdam, Van, 39
Maastricht, 28
Mabuse, Jan Gossaert van, 8
Mackay, 48
Margaretha of York, 6
Margaretha, heiress of Lodewyck
  of Male, 4
Margaretha of Parma, the
  Governess, 11, 14
Maria, Duchess of Burgundy, 7
Marlborough, 32
Mathias, Archduke of Habsburg,
  Governor, 13
Maurits, Johan of Nassau, 21
Maurits, Prince, son of William of
  Orange, 15, 16, 17, 18, 19, 20
Maximilian of Habsburg, German
  Emperor, 7, 8
Metsijs, Quenten, 8
Monk, English Admiral, 26
Montigny, 10
Multatuli, 46
Mussert, A. A., 53

Napoleon, Emperor, 38, 39, 40
Napoleon, III, 46
Nassau, Justinus van, 16
Neck, Jacob van, 17
Nieuwenhuis, Domela F., 47,
  48
Nijevelt, Van Zuylen van, 46
Noort, Oliver van, 17
Nybjorg, Admiral, 25

Obdam, Van Wassenaar, 26
Oldenbarnevelt, Johan van, 15,
  17, 19, 20
Orly, Barend van, 8

Peter the Great, Czar of Russia,
  31
Philip of Anjou, 31, 32
Philip the Bold of Burgundy, 4, 6
Philip the Fair, Duke of Habsburg,
  7, 8
Philip the Good of Burgundy, 5, 6
Phillip II of Habsburg, King of
  Spain, 10, 11, 13, 14, 15, 16, 17

Philip IV, King of France, 3
Pierson, Minister, 48, 49
Pippin II, 1
Plancius, 17
Potieter, 43
Ptolemy, 22

Quay, de, 62

Radbod, Frisian King, 1
Rappard, van, 45
Requesens, Spanish Governor, 13
Richelieu, 20
Riebeeck, Jan van, 24
Roentgen, G.M., 40
Roggeveen, Jacob, 33
Rupert, English Admiral, 26
Ruyter, Admiral de, 25, 26, 28,
  29

Schaper, 48
Schermerhorn, 53, 57
Schimmelpenninck, 36, 38
Scholte of Doeveren, 43
Schouten, Willem, 19
Scorel, Jan van, 8
Seyss-Inquart, 55
Simonsz, Menno, 9
Snijders, General C.J., 50
Speelman, Cornelis, 26
Spinola, General, 20
Spronck, Martinus, 20
Stanley, 15
Starkenborch-Stachouwer, Tjarda
  van, Gov. Gen., 56
Steven, van der Haghen, 17
Stikker, D.U., 62
Stuart, Mary, daughter of King
  Charles I of England, 22, 29,
  30
Stuvysant, Pieter, 25
Sukarno, 53, 57, 64

Tasman, Abel, 22
Thorbecke, 44, 45, 47
Troelstra, 48, 51
Tromp, Dutch Admiral, 23, 24

Uytenbogaert, 18

Verhulst, Willem, 20
Vetter, General, 48
Voes, Hendrik, 9
Vreede, Pieter, 37

Waal, De, 47
Warfuse, 21
Welter, 54
Wenceslas, Duke of Brabant, 4
Westerling, Captain, 58
Widukind, King of Saxons, 1
Wilhelm, Kaiser, 51, 52
Wilhelmina of Belgium, Queen,
   54
Wilhelmina of Orange, Queen,
   47, 48, 49, 52, 55, 56, 59, 62
Wilhelmina, Princess, wife of
   William V, 36
William I, 39, 40, 42, 43
William, Duke of Guelders and
   Cleves, 9
William, Prince, son of Frederick
   Henry, 22, 23
William I of Orange, King, 10, 11,
   12, 13, 14, 15
William II, Count of Holland, 3
William VI, Count of Holland, 5
William II, Frederick, King of
   Prussia, 36
William II, son of William I, 44,
   45
William III, of Orange, 23, 25,
   27, 28, 29, 30, 32, 33
William III, son of William II,
   45, 46, 48
William IV, 33, 34
William V, 34, 35, 36, 38
Willibrord, 1
Willoughby, 15
Witt, Johan de, 24, 25, 26, 28

York, 15
York, Duke of, 26

Zuylestein, 25